Richard & Ann,

Just a few snaps of 'our back yard'....

Look forward to showing you around

love
Andrew & Lynne xo

Christmas 2003

Mornington Peninsula
Sea Breeze and Sand

foreword by Dame Elisabeth Murdoch AC DBE

Anne Monteith and Bryce Dunkley

Ides Publishing

AUSTRALIA
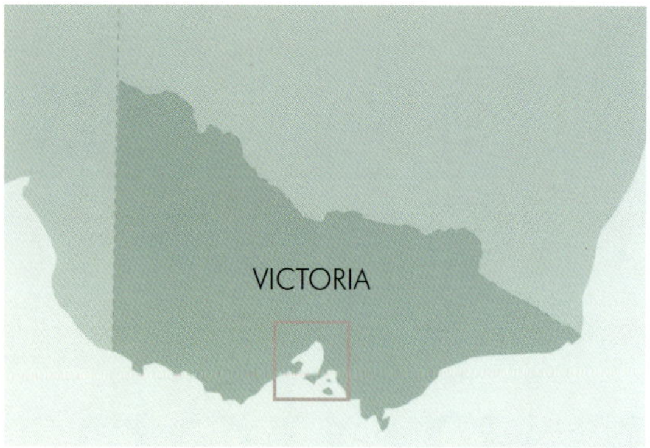
VICTORIA

MELBOURNE

PORT PHILLIP BAY
THE RIP
MORNINGTON PENINSULA
WESTERN PORT BAY
Mount Eliza
Mornington
Mount Martha
Safety Beach
Dromana
McCrae
Rosebud
Tootgarook
Rye
Blairgowrie
Sorrento
Portsea
Point Nepean
Portsea Surf Beach
Sorrento Back Beach
Bay of Islands
Koonya
Montforts
Bridgewater Bay
Pirates Bay
The Divide
Number Sixteen
Rye Ocean Beach
St Andrews
Gunnamatta
Cape Schanck
Bushrangers Bay
Blowhole
Flinders
Shoreham
Point Leo
Merricks
Balnarring
Somers
Cerberus
Stony Point
Hastings

Contents

FOREWORD
by Dame Elisabeth Murdoch AC DBE iv

INTRODUCTION v

Port Phillip Bay 8

BAY BEACHES
| Mount Eliza 16
| Mornington 20
| Mount Martha 28
| Safety Beach 35
| Dromana 38
| McCrae 46
| Rosebud 50
| Tootgarook 56
| Rye 58
| Blairgowrie 66
| Sorrento 72
| Portsea 92

Point Nepean 101
The Rip 106

OCEAN BEACHES
| Portsea 110
| Sorrento 117
| Bay of Islands 123
| Koonya 126
| Blairgowrie 128
| Pirates Bay 129
| Montforts 130
| Bridgewater Bay 132
| The Divide 136
| Number Sixteen 138
| Rye 139
| St Andrews 142
| Gunnamatta 144
| Cape Schanck 146

Hinterland 152

WESTERN PORT BEACHES
| Flinders 160
| Shoreham 163
| Point Leo 166
| Merricks 170
| Balnarring 171
| Somers 173
| Cerberus 178
| Stony Point 180
| Hastings 183

Foreword

Welcome to *Sea Breeze and Sand*, a great treat for all who love our beautiful Mornington Peninsula. It helps us to know, understand and appreciate in full the treasures which encircle the Mornington Peninsula; though quite a small piece of Victoria, it is one of the most interesting parts of our state. It is historically and visually very rich.

Bryce Dunkley's photography is superb and Anne Monteith has covered the whole area with fascinating history about each of the areas and people who live in them.

Warmest congratulations to Anne Monteith and Bryce Dunkley; as we look at and enjoy *Sea Breeze and Sand*, we must be very thankful to them and I am very honoured to have been invited to write the foreword.

Dame Elisabeth Murdoch AC DBE

Introduction

Melburnians have a strong affection for the Mornington Peninsula. Its memories include generations of summer holidays - possibly camping on the foreshore or staying in a rented fibro shack, while for some it is a playground for the wealthy where the highway ends at Sorrento and Portsea.

For others, the Peninsula offers frequent weekend getaways. It is a rich mosaic of golf courses and vineyards, restaurants and markets, historic homesteads and marine parks, farms and seaside villages, native flora and fauna - and many beaches.

But which beach? A quiet sandy strip dotted with colourful bathing boxes on Port Phillip Bay, or a brisk walk to admire the surf-ravaged coastline near Cape Schanck, or perhaps a more scientific stroll among the mangroves and pelicans at the northern end of Western Port Bay? For the casual visitor the options are almost overwhelming. But even the frequent visitor or permanent resident would be hard-pressed to enjoy all that the Peninsula has to offer.

Sea Breeze and Sand is a coastal tour. The starting point is Port Phillip Bay, Melbourne's maritime playground. From the comfort of Mount Eliza we journey southward enjoying the many charming beaches from Mornington to Rosebud and Tootgarook to Sorrento, the location of a brief unsuccessful settlement in 1803.

From the cafes of Sorrento and its affluent neighbour Portsea, to historic Point Nepean and evidence of its former roles in defence and immigration. Between Point Nepean and Point Lonsdale lies the Heads, the narrow entrance to Port Phillip Bay and the notorious Rip.

Outside the Heads, Bass Strait provides a stark contrast to the vast serenity of Port Phillip Bay. The wild ocean beaches of Portsea, Rye and Gunnamatta are spectacular and treacherous and the many shipwrecks are testament to this. Evocative titles hint at the nature of each seascape ... Bushrangers Bay, Dogs Head, London Bridge, and Bay of Islands.

Continuing on our anti-clockwise journey, the Cape Schanck Lighthouse interrupts the long stretch of yellow sands and limestone cliffs which transform dramatically to black, basalt headlands as we proceed to the east. Western Port Bay's `coast of coves´ begins at the fishing village of Flinders and includes the quiet picturesque beaches of the southern bay with their views across to Phillip Island.

From Stony Point to Hastings the coastline displays a distinctively commercial and industrial character. But still there is more. At the northern end of Western Port Bay is a region of internationally significant marine and coastal ecosystems, of extensive mangroves which are exposed along the mud flats at low tide.

Sea Breeze and Sand is a photographic record of a journey around the coastline of the Mornington Peninsula, complemented by snippets of history and geography and the opportunity to meet an eclectic mix of local people. Some were chance meetings; others keenly sought. All contribute meaningfully to a place for which they are fiercely loyal.

The people of the Mornington Peninsula are many and varied - retirees and farmers, environmentalists and summer campers, artists and wine lovers, from the industrial zone on the edge of the metropolis to the spectacular cliff-top dwellings at the southern tip - all share a common affection, a bond with their own favourite part of the Peninsula. Through these people *Sea Breeze and Sand* seeks to reflect the vibrant, diverse communities on the Peninsula and capture the distinctive character of each seaside town.

The Mornington Peninsula is about infinite contrast - quiet bays and powerful ocean, crowded and deserted seascapes, summer sunshine and winter fog, surf fishing and bushwalking, dolphins and kangaroos, images of the iconic and unusual, contemporary times and bygone eras.

Enjoy your journey through the Mornington Peninsula as you are welcomed by the *Sea Breeze and Sand*.

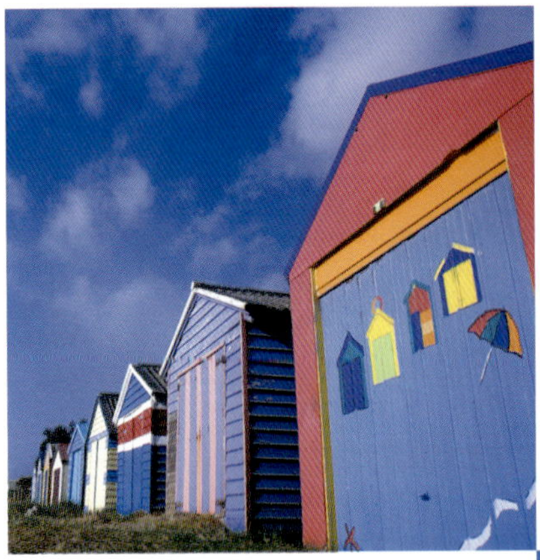

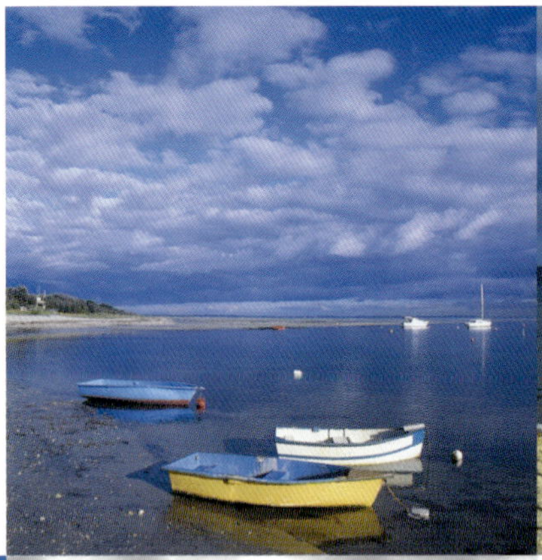

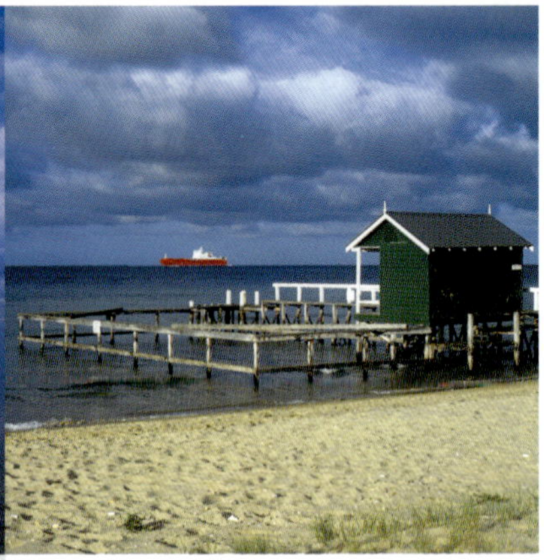

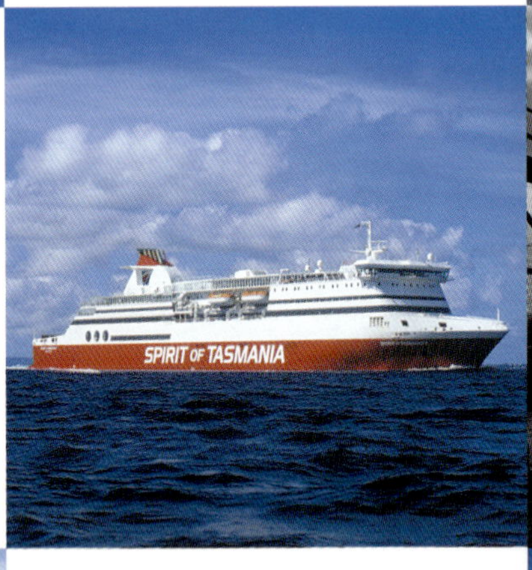
SPIRIT OF TASMANIA

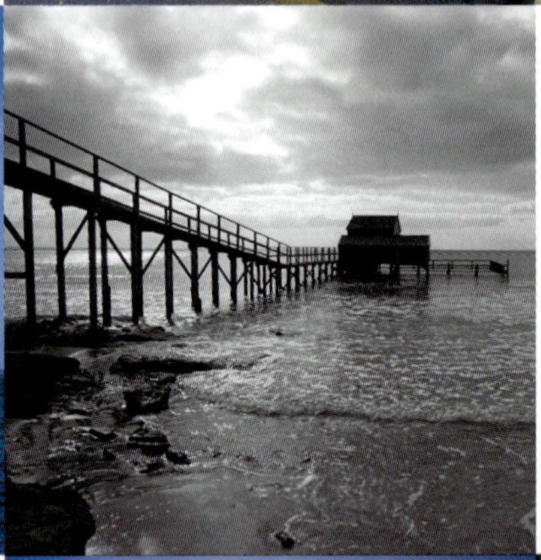

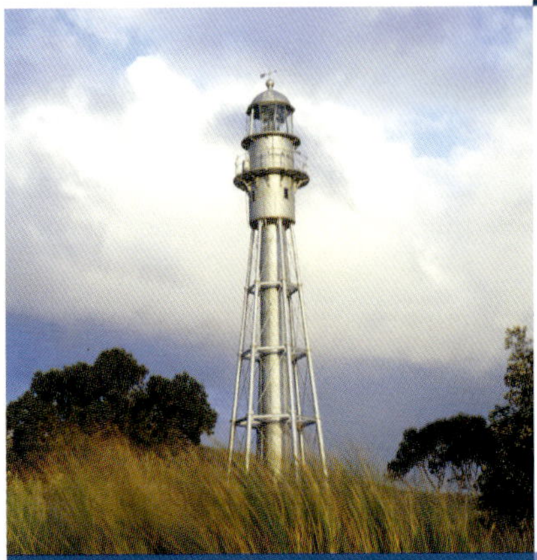

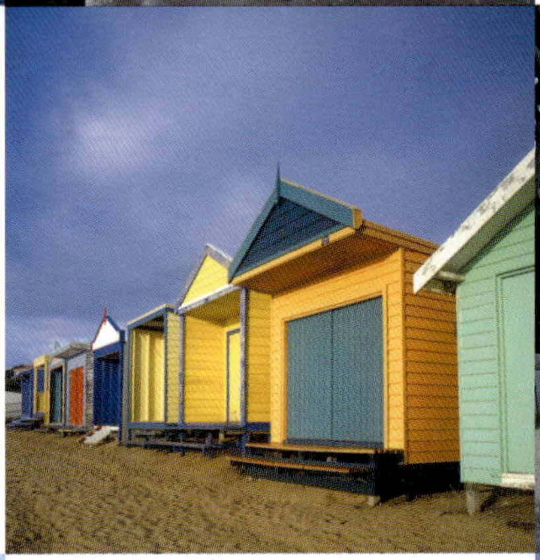

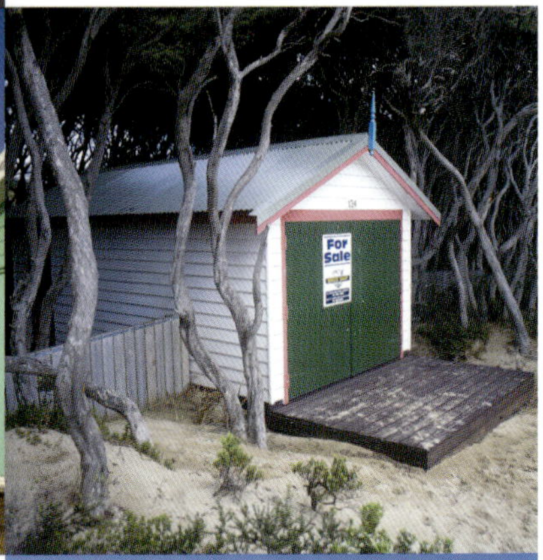
For Sale

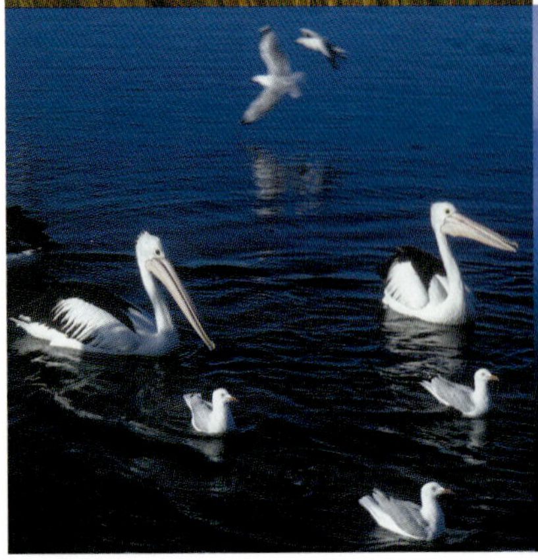

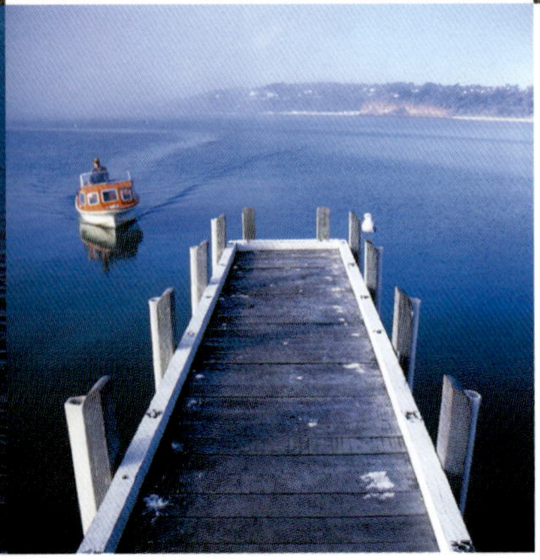

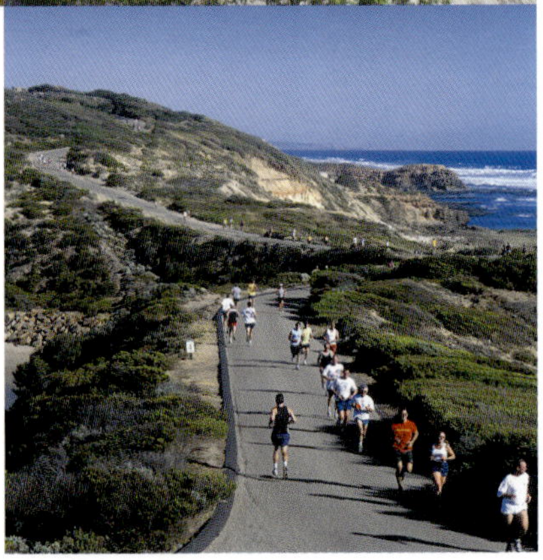

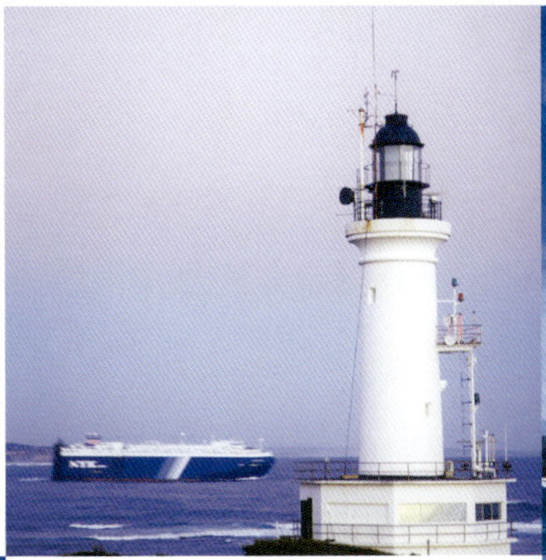
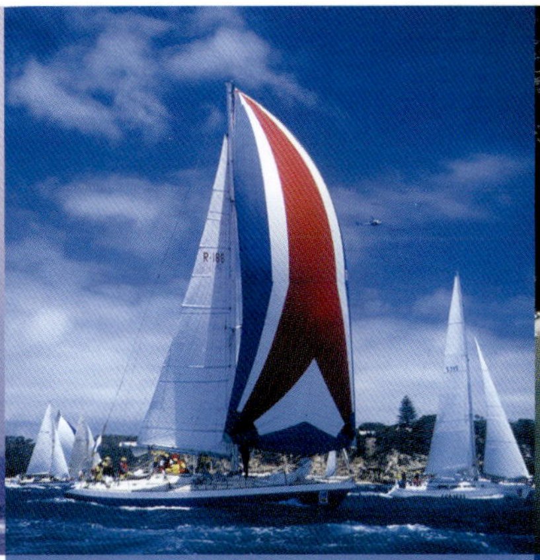
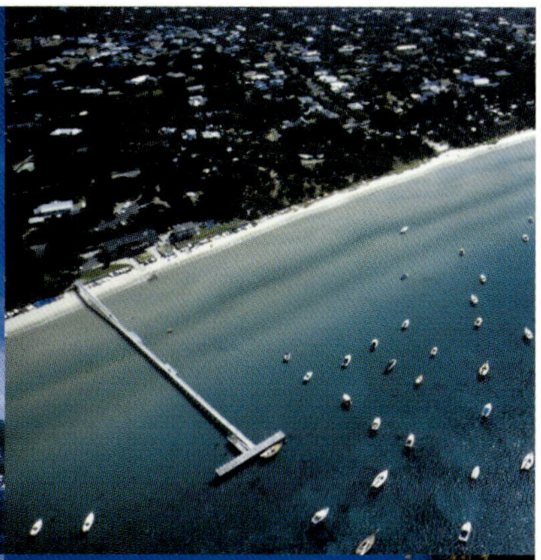
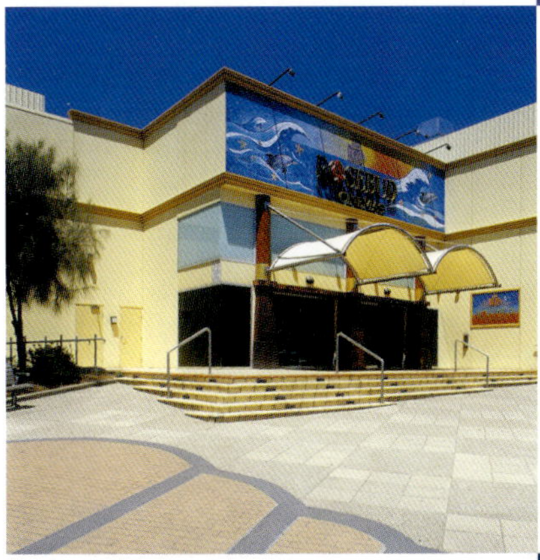
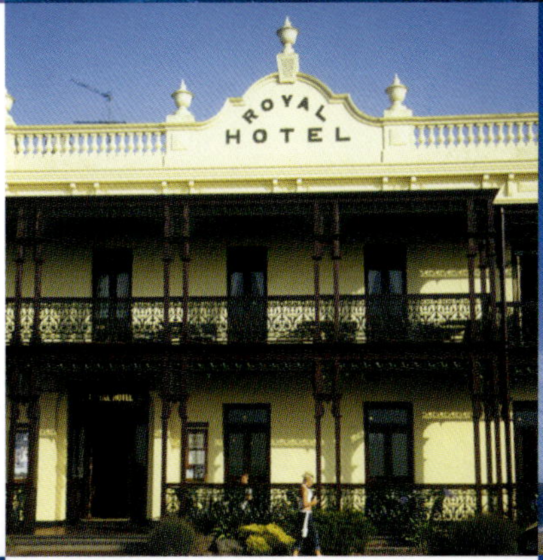
ROYAL
HOTEL
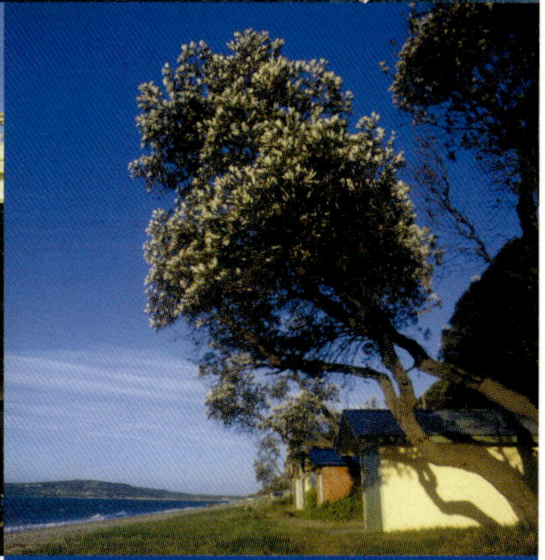

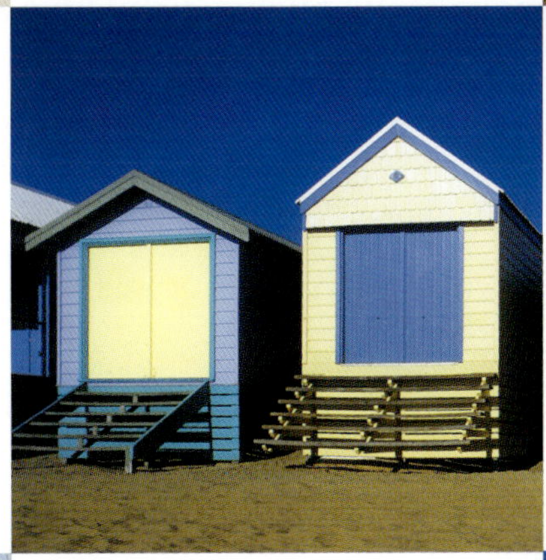
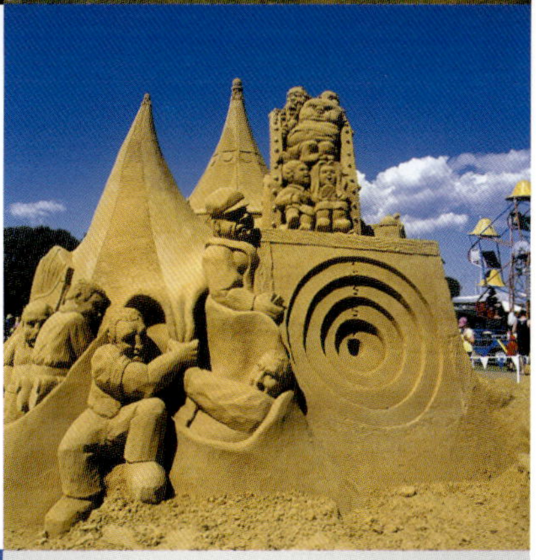
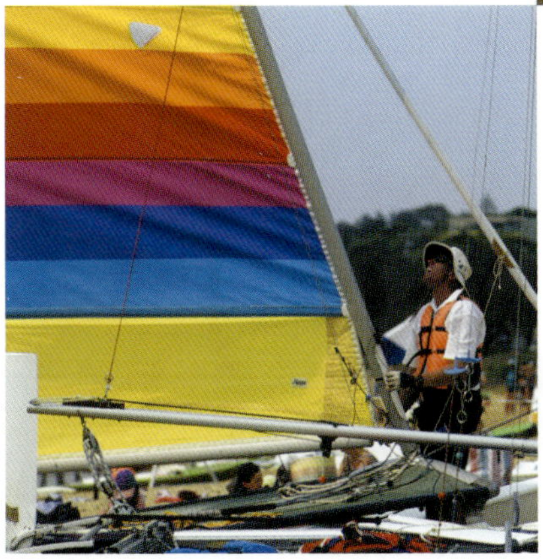
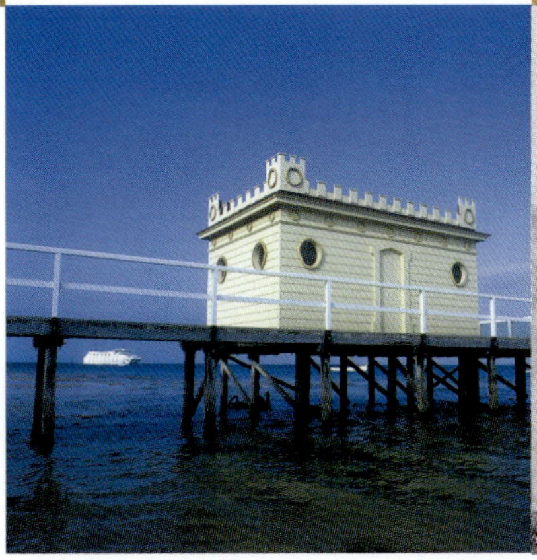
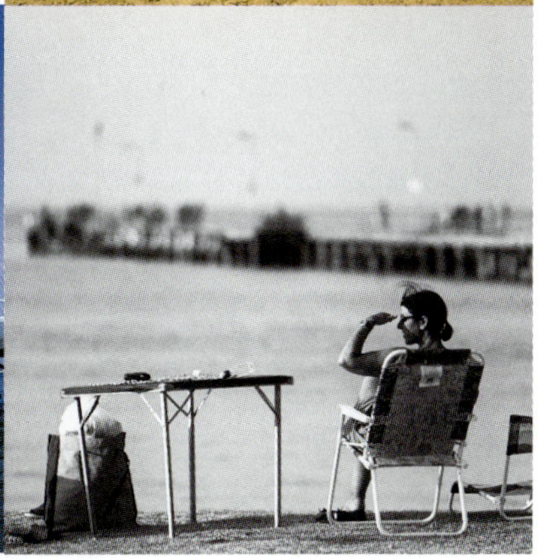

Port Phillip Bay

Port Phillip Bay is an integral part of Peninsula lifestyle and culture - a haven for boating enthusiasts, windsurfers, anglers and swimmers. It has over 3.2 million people living around its shores and is the gateway to Victoria's two largest cities Melbourne and Geelong. The bay is thirty-five times larger than Sydney Harbour. The notorious entrance, called `The Rip´, is reputed to be one of the most treacherous stretches of water in the world, claiming more than 130 ships within ten nautical miles of the Heads.

The bay is named after Captain Arthur Phillip who was the first governor of New South Wales. He was the captain of the First Fleet that brought the original settlers and convicts to Australia from England in 1788.

Port Phillip Bay is dotted with small islands, historical bay defences, shipwrecks and more than 150 navigation aids, lighthouses, markers, beacons and buoys which mark the shipping channels. The waters of Port Phillip Heads receive more than 7000 ship-visits annually including cargo vessels, coastal traders, cruise ships and large container ships.

The main shipping channel is aligned underwater with the ancient course of the Yarra River. It follows the eastern coastline turning sharply at the Hovell Pile, which marks the entrance to the South Channel. Elsewhere is too shallow. From here the ships complete a ninety-degree turn, then proceed to Melbourne or Geelong. Standing on the Rosebud Pier enables a close view of this sharp manoeuvre. From Arthur's Seat on a clear day, it is possible to view a ship's entire progress from Melbourne to the Heads.

South Channel Marker - Number 4

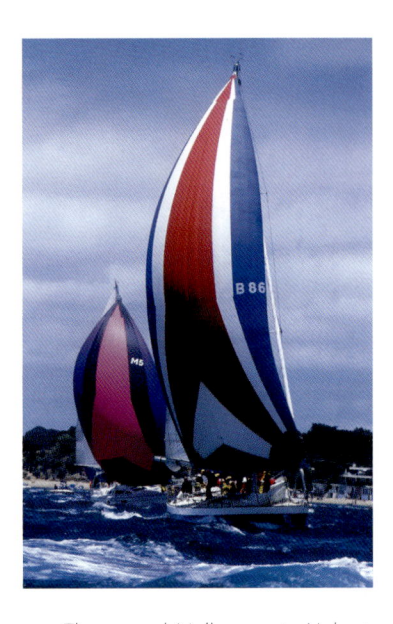

The annual Melbourne to Hobart Yacht Race

Queenscliff - Sorrento vehicular ferry

South Cardinal Marker - Popes Eye

PORT PHILLIP BAY

The 'red-and-white Twins' are becoming bay icons. Spirit of Tasmania I and II make daily crossings between Melbourne and Devonport, taking ten hours and carrying up to 1000 passengers and 650 vehicles each.

Gannets

Over 70 species of birds are found in Port Phillip Bay. The Australasian Diving Gannet is a large seabird which dives vertically from a height up to thirty metres entering the water at tremendous speeds. The largest colony of these birds is at Popes Eye. They breed in Port Phillip Bay where they take advantage of the nesting sites offered by navigational beacons and channel markers.

Small colonies of Australian Fur Seals occupy the navigational structures that border the Bay's shipping channels. The male seals can grow to 2.3 metres.

Australian Fur Seal

Chinamans Hut

Meet Judy Muir

POLPERRO DOLPHIN SWIMS

Judy Muir is warmly regarded as the Dolphin Lady. The Muir family has owned and operated Polperro Dolphin Swims for more than 18 years. It is an environmental tourism operation that offers the opportunity to observe and swim with wild bottlenose dolphins in Port Phillip Bay.

Judy is at home in the sea and was one of the first women to swim the infamous Rip in 1998. Judy swam alongside dolphins when training for long distance open-water swims and was captivated by their graceful movement and sense of fun. The resident population of more than one hundred bottlenose dolphins congregate in the southern end of the bay over summer. Stable weather conditions and prolific fish stocks make this area ideal for nursery groups to rear their young.

The Dolphin Research Institute has been studying the dolphins in the bay since the late 1980's and approached the Muirs because of their interest in running dolphin swims. The Institute was intrigued by the dolphins' apparent attraction to the *Polperro* and became a means to promote and fund research.

With the seaside community rapidly transforming, Judy Muir is concerned about the increased use of the bay and the `theme park dilemma´. She is proud that *Polperro's* commercial success has been achieved within environmental limits. Judy is heavily involved in the community through her visits to schools, support for local tourism and aquatic organizations and she was awarded the Australian Sports Medal Award in 2000. When asked about her qualifications, Judy replied, `Two arms, two legs and a heart that beats with a passion for the marine environment and all that Nature sustains´.

Photo courtesy Troy Muir, Polperrro Dolphin Swims

South Channel Fort

The Fort was built in the 1880's in a triangle of defence with Point Nepean and Queenscliff. It is a small artificial island of about 0.7 hectares built up on bluestone boulders, concrete and sand. Its main purpose was to illuminate the channel at night and to electronically explode mines under the attacking ships should they breach the heavily fortified Port Phillip Heads. In its heyday 100 officers lived and worked on the island. The Fort contains antiquated gun emplacements, a labyrinth of underground passages and magnificent views over Port Phillip Bay. It is a vital breeding site for the vulnerable White-faced Storm-Petrel.

South Channel Pile Light

For 111 years the South Channel Pile Light guided ships through the narrow shipping channel. The single story octagonal structure was built in 1872. It is nine metres wide and stands on timber piles in the water.

The kerosene-fired light was tended by live-in lightkeepers. It was a lonely life for most, but sometimes families of up to four lived in the tiny cottage for months at a time. The cottage has a living room, a bedroom with four narrow bunks, a storeroom and a small, spiral staircase. Two water tanks stored rainwater collected from the roof. Large ships would dwarf the structure as they passed but none ever hit the lighthouse. Keepers would wait for a passenger ferry to pass each morning to receive the newspaper that was tossed from the deck.

The last light keeper left in 1925 when the introduction of bottled acetylene gas as fuel for the light made the job redundant. In 1985 the light was switched off for a trial and never turned on again. From this time the condition of the building deteriorated from lack of maintenance. In 1998 the structure, the only one of its kind intact in Australia, was lifted off the original piles and transported to a shed on South Wharf where it was restored and painted. It was relocated safely out of the shipping channel, about three kilometres away from its original location.

Meet Jack (John) Mackeddie
MANAGING DIRECTOR, PENINSULA SEAROAD TRANSPORT

The two white vehicular ferries are synonymous with the southern end of Port Phillip Bay. Each can carry eighty cars and seven hundred passengers between Sorrento and Queenscliff. The first ferry to cross the bay linking the Mornington and Bellarine Peninsulas was the *Peninsula Princess* in 1987. Before then it was necessary to travel two hundred kilometres on land to cover ten kilometres on water. There were many battles, complex planning requirements, submissions and appeals to enable this service to be established.

The *MV Queenscliff* replaced the old ferry in 1993. Jack Mackeddie was instrumental in its research and design and worked to secure outstanding passenger facilities aboard. The people of the company had made their dream come true: here was a vehicular ferry and terminal facilities that Victorians could show off with pride.

In 2001 the *MV Sorrento* was added to the service enabling crossings every hour. It is Jack Mackeddie's pride and joy. The ferry was built in Tasmania with Jack as the project manager. Both ferries have been purpose built for use in Port Phillip Bay and are not dependent on weather conditions.

Jack Mackeddie's story is one of enormous frustration, frantic work and incredible spirit. He has a sense of pride and achievement and considers his ferries to be a vital part of the road network. Jack is grateful to the people he employs, `the people are the company´, and he maintains that `the success of the ferries are proof that responsible development can exist within areas of natural beauty´.

Jack and his crews recount the variety of passengers and cargo that has been dispatched over the years: fire trucks attending bushfires, koalas and penguins being relocated, racehorses on route to the track, cattle trucks, palm trees, coaches on tour and cyclists in the `Around the Bay´ ride. Commuters and tourists account for the regular patronage. On the bayside of the Southern Peninsula these ferries provide a source of interest and a comforting familiarity.

PORT PHILLIP BAY

Ferry crossing from Queenscliff to Sorrento

MV Sorrento and MV Queenscliff

Mount Eliza

Journeying to the southeast from Melbourne, Mount Eliza is the northern-most bayside town on the Mornington Peninsula. It is distinguishable by its lush native vegetation, coastal cliffs and sandy beaches that include Daveys Bay, Canadian Bay, Half Moon Bay, Ranelagh, Moondah and Sunnyside. The village shops are stylish with an image of exclusivity and many grand residences grace this prestigious suburb.

Mount Eliza has been described as the South Yarra of the Peninsula. Some quotable quotes from residents include -
`We don't mind if everyone else just drives past and leaves us in peace´. `It is like living between a badly behaved adolescent on one side and a playground on the other!´ `It took a while to become part of the community but when you eventually do, it is a fantastic place to live. Don't tell everyone - we want to keep it a secret!´

In 1946 James Davey, one of Mount Eliza's first landowners, took up a squatter's licence for the land between the shore and Nepean Highway. *Davey's Bay* is surrounded by eroding cliffs and has an air of secrecy. The path along the cliff top leads to countless steps discreetly emerging at the yacht club. The absence of people is no surprise given its limited access and sense of isolation.

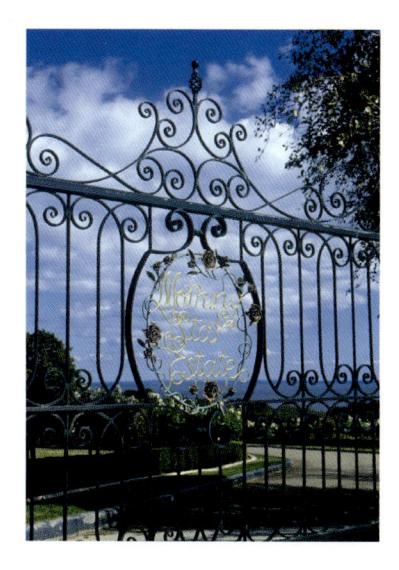

MOUNT ELIZA

Morning Star Estate. The large manor dates back to the 1860's having had many uses including a boys' home. It now includes a restaurant, cellar door, boutique hotel and conference facility set in superb gardens with spectacular views of Port Phillip Bay.

Toorak College. Originally located in Toorak, Victoria's oldest independent girls' school dates back to 1854. The prestigious boarding school moved to Mount Eliza in 1928.

Moondah Estate (1888) was once described as a `palace by the sea'. In 1947 it became the exclusive Hotel Manyung and since 1957, the renowned Mount Eliza Business School.

Mount Eliza Beaches

Beach box number 69

Ranelagh Beach

Mount Eliza's bays and beaches have derived their names from early settlers to the area. *Canadian Bay* was named after three Canadian lumbermen who operated a sawmill in the 1850's. The abundant timber - mainly gum, wattle and sheoak - was highly sought after in Melbourne.

In the 1950's this bay became famous for the filming of Neville Shute's classic, `On The Beach´ and Ava Gardner's legendary comment `that´s the place for it´ - her purported reaction to setting a film in Melbourne about the end of the world.

Ranelagh Beach is a popular sandy beach with colourful beach boxes. Ranelagh Estate, with its pattern of curved streets was established in the 1920's. Walter Burley Griffin, designer of Canberra, Australia's capital city, was also associated with that design. Streets were named after places around the London suburb of Wimbledon. The Ranelagh Club was established in 1927 exclusively for Estate landowners. Today membership is available for Mornington Peninsula residents.

MOUNT ELIZA

Ranelagh Beach in winter

Mornington

Mornington, originally named Schnapper Point, is the largest town on the Peninsula. With a naturally deep harbour it had origins as a fishing village later becoming a favourite holiday destination for Melburnians travelling there by horse and cart or paddlesteamer. The town's activities have always centred around Mornington Park which was officially set aside as a reserve in 1874 to be used for `promenade and recreation´. The familiar stone entrances were built during the 1930's economic depression.

From the timbered cliff tops of Beleura Hill the coastline forms a bay with sandy beaches and red bluffs culminating in the picturesque harbour. Beautiful historical buildings reflect life in a bygone era. It is a stylish seaside town with a distinctly maritime atmosphere.

Mornington Pier

MORNINGTON

Mornington Harbour towards Mills Beach and Red Bluff Point

Sunrise, Mornington Harbour

Mornington Beaches

The six Mornington beaches have distinguishing features. Mills Beach has the vibrant beach boxes and Life Saving Club while Shire Hall was renowned for its fishermen's huts dating back to the 1850's. Scout Hall Beach has a backdrop of striking red cliffs and Mother's Beach is protected by the pier and considered safe for young children. Royal Beach, with old stone steps and a fraying sea wall, is named after the hotel on the cliffs above it and Fossil Beach has the remains of limeburners' kilns.

Mills Beach

Meet The Hutchins Brothers
FIFTH GENERATION FISHING FAMILY

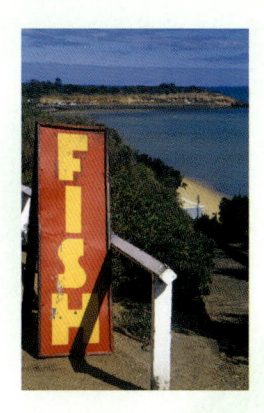

The Hutchins family has been fishing since 1860. The name is associated with Mornington, McCrae, Mount Martha and Blairgowrie. The jetty at Cameron's Bight, Sorrento is named after them. When the brothers were young their parents laid them in fishing boxes while they sold fresh fish from their shop on the beach.

Driving along the Esplanade above Fisherman's Beach a red-and-yellow sign will attest to the fishing activities of Neville and Dalton who fish most days. Their brother Kevin joins them on weekends. Most of the fish are caught within 200 metres of the shoreline and includes flathead, whiting, flounder, salmon, mullet and garfish.

When Neville spies schools of fish from the cliff top he uses a walkie-talkie to instruct Dalton where to manoeuvre his boat to encourage the fish into the mesh nets. The brothers use large nets that allow smaller fish to swim free. They monitor each catch and are careful to return undersized fish. Preserving fish stocks is crucial to the viability of their business. They are conscious of only taking what they can sell locally.

The fresh fish is sold from their rudimentary, but large and comfortably appointed blue shed on `Fishy's Beach´. It was built by their late grandfather who used timber washed ashore from container vessels. It was extended in the 1940's by their father and is now classified by the National Trust.

The phrase `salt of the earth´ could have been coined for these gentlemen. It is worth the trip to meet the rugged and congenial Hutchins brothers and purchase their reasonably priced fish that is guaranteed to be fresh.

Beleura

This Italianate villa was erected in 1863 for James Butchart pastoralist. Purchased by Charles Edward Bright founder of Bright brothers & Co. Steamship & General Agents and then used as a summer retreat by his father-in-law, the Viscount Canterbury, KCB, Governor of Victoria (1866-1873). Enlarged in 1883 by the Hon. Caleb Joshua Jenner Member of the Legislative Council of The Parliament of Victoria, merchant and banker. Acquired in 1899 by Robert Smith Esq pastoralist and later sold to William Ernest Albert Edwick grazier.

Purchased by Silent Showman Sir George Tallis, KCB, theatrical entrepreneur, gentleman farmer and pastoralist and Amelia, Lady Tallis actress, doyen of Melbourne society and charity worker, Beleura was used as the family's seaside house - (1916-1948). In 1948 by family agreement, Beleura was acquired by the youngest son, John Tallis, gentleman composer of music, musician, historian and gardener. Beleura was bequeathed by him to the people of Victoria in 1996 as a tribute to George and Lady Tallis.

Part of the bequest it is rumoured, includes the lifelong care of the family pet leading to a popular local myth that the estate was left to a dog. The magnificent home and gardens can be visited by appointment.

Meet Milton Green
MORNINGTON RESIDENT

Bluestone gutters. Verandah posts. Blacksmiths in Mornington's main-street. Professional fishermen in the harbour. Six flathead for a shilling. Milk and groceries delivered by horse and cart. Picnics in the Park. Sennetts icecream. Melbourne day-trippers arriving in Mornington travelling in furniture removal vans with platform seats, a billy of boiling water included in the cost. These are Milton's memories of the Forties.

The War ended. Migrants arrived and assimilated well. Milton, at Rosebud High School, recalls the head prefect - a girl gifted in arts and journalism, with exotic lunches - Stephanie Alexander, alongside the Lacos, Croads and Skeltons. Milton left Mornington seeking employment, but later returned with his own family and fulfilled a dream of a home at Beleura Hill. He displays a genuine fondness for Mornington, the backdrop for his life's highlights - his family and sailing.

At fifteen years of age, Milton went to the 1956 Olympics in Melbourne with the Sea Scouts in a patrol boat. Watching New Zealand win the gold medal was one of the highlights. Milton loves sailing Couta boats and rates himself as a `fair average quality sailor´. When asked how he developed this passion he replied, `Swimming and sailing to a child growing up in Mornington was as natural as riding horses or handling guns on a farm´.

Why Couta boats? As fate would have it, in 1984 a huge storm caused severe damage to boats at Mornington, including Milton's. On a beautiful Australia Day weekend the Mornington Yacht Club fleet sailed to Geelong for a Regatta and the Sorrento Couta boats used the Mornington moorings. Milton fell in love with the line-up of those elegant traditional fishing boats. He could not resist having his own Couta boat built and he named it in the tradition of fishermen after his mother Jessie. The tradition continued when Milton´s first granddaughter was born on his mother's ninety-first birthday. She, too, was named Jessie - more of life's joys.

In the 1988 Bicentenial celebrations, six Couta boats went to Sydney to compete in the biennial Old Gaffers Regatta. `Jessie won! International journalists covering the event threw the Aussies a challenge, threatening to `sail our pants off´! Australia took it up and sent Jessie as deck cargo to Belgium then overland across France. We showed what Australian sailors could do and cleaned-up by winning the boat-handling competition´.

Milton attributes his enjoyment of life to role models in the sailing community, his family and the Peninsula environment. These also helped him overcome setbacks. Milton has a commitment to giving back to the town that he loves and works quietly behind the scenes as a mentor and role model for others. He recalls his mother saying that community service is rent that we pay for time on earth. Milton would `rather wear out, not rust out´.

Milton Green on board his Couta boat Jessie

Australia Day Parade, January 26

Main Street, Mornington

Mornington Cup

The first meeting of the Mornington Racing Club was in 1899. Racing was suspended during World War Two and the army used the grounds as a training camp. The Club promotes itself as `more than a racing club´. *City racing with a country feel*. It is now one of the premier country racecourses in the state and the annual Cup meeting, held in mid February is Mornington´s biggest day.

Mount Martha

Timeless popularity. Mount Martha is one of the prettiest settlements on the bay. The Esplanade links several small beaches - Dava, Birdrock, Craigie and Hawker. North and South Beaches then provide elongated stretches of sand famous for their colourful clusters of beach boxes. A scenic drive continues for six kilometres winding its way along dramatic cliff tops from which can be seen anglers perched on rugged ledges and swimmers diving or snorkelling below.

Birdrock Beach

MOUNT MARTHA

Hobie sailing has been a way of life for catamaran sailors for more than thirty years. It is said that Hobie sailors are as colourful as the boats they own and adore.

'The Pillars' is the local name given to the popular spot for jumping or diving from the cliffs at Mount Martha.

Balcombe Point

MOUNT MARTHA

Anglers at sunset

Dromana

Dromana is located at the foot of Arthurs Seat where `the mountain meets the sea´. The seaside town has provided a strong link with the hinterland district and the original pier was built in 1862 to enable the exchange of produce, especially timber. Tourists arrived by paddlesteamer, attracted by the bay and bush location.

In the 1940's Dromana became one of the first foreshores to attract campers in `tent cities´. From the 1960's the famous chairlift operated from the Arthurs Seat Summit enabling visitors to experience panoramic views of Port Phillip Bay. Dromana is the start of the Two Bays Walking Track which winds through forest and woodlands providing teasing glimpses of ocean scenery on route to Cape Schanck.

The hub of the town's activity is retail shopping that has developed along Point Nepean Road. Well-maintained lawns are a feature of the foreshore with trees that tell a story of prevailing winds.

Dromana foreshore

Winter's long stretch of deserted beach and lonely bathing boxes are transformed in summer by colourful umbrellas, beach towels and sunning bodies.

Dromana's sandy beach stretches from the pier to Anthonys Nose.

Meet Ernie Jackson
DROMANA FORESHORE CAMPER

Three generations of this family annually camp on the Dromana Foreshore Reserve. It is as strong as tradition gets. Ernie brought his children here on holidays 47 years ago. With daughter Sandra and granddaughter Dana, they epitomize the camping culture of many families who return year after year to the same location. Camping styles have progressed from the simple tent to a caravan, adding the annexe and luxuries of home - microwave oven, refrigerator, television. Lifelong friendships have been forged and many girls have married the boy down the beach.

There are sixty caravans here and a waiting list. Sites only become available with natural attrition. It is a prime location - close to the beach, a boat ramp, with no road to cross, safe for children and everyone looks out for each other. The campers are actively involved in preserving the area, with working bees and vegetation maintenance.

Ernie Jackson loves the peace, the fishing and his old friends. He stays from December to Easter and `keeps an eye on´ everyone else's site when they are not there. `Everyone treats each other equally. There are rich and poor here and no one is treated differently. It is a sense of community. In town, people don´t know their neighbours´.

Sandra says everyone gets along with each other and nicknames over the years have evolved. She speaks fondly of their `friends in the Chardonnay Set, their Wog Mates, the Liberals and the amazing Gypsy Point residents´. All fun. `And everyone teaches everyone else to water ski or perfect their camping techniques´.

Dana speaks on behalf of the teenage residents. She says they love spending the days on the beach and walking to the cinema or shops in Rosebud. `We look forward to our summer friends´. Everyone feels safe in the water when the campers are around. The conditions on the bay can change rapidly and many times assistance has been required to retrieve stranded boat users from the water. `No one hesitates if help is required´.

`Anthonys Nose´ is the distinctive section of the Point Nepean Road where the granite hillside meets the sea, effectively breaking the ribbon pattern of coastal development. The cutting of the road around 1866 ended the isolation that the southern seaside towns experienced over winter. Access by land had been extremely difficult until then. Even now there are times when waves crash fiercely against the retaining rocks and onto the road.

Three generations

Arthurs Seat

Arthurs Seat is the highest point (304metres) on the Mornington Peninsula. It is set in a State Park and commands panoramic views of Port Phillip and Westernport Bays as well as Phillip Island and French Island. Countless piers and jetties can be seen along the sandy foreshores to the south while red cliffs abruptly interrupt the landscape to the north. Ships and navigation beacons dot the bay. Franklin Point, Murrays Lookout and Chapman Point are spectacular vantage points to view the setting sun.

DROMANA

Matthew Flinders Cairn

Matthew Flinders was the first European to climb Arthurs Seat. His ship, the *Investigator*, entered the Heads while making a circumnavigation of Australia in 1802. The Matthew Flinders Cairn commemorates his climb and is located on the upper slopes of Arthurs Seat a short distance below Chapman's Point.

McCrae

McCrae is a small and charming township. The beach has fine white sand which contrasts against the aquamarine water. `The kind of beach that is invisible to passing traffic - a secret we treasure´.

McCrae Beach

Meet Phil Fowler

RANGER IN CHARGE, EASTERN BAY

Phil Fowler manages Port Phillip Bay from Portsea pier to Brighton. He has responsibilities up to the high water mark including five metres around each pier. Part of his job involves looking after navigational and recreational markers, boating and ski access zones and marine parks. Phil was the last lighthouse keeper at the Eastern Lighthouse, McCrae. The lighthouse is no longer operational. In 1994 Phil had the task of turning off the light for the last time, no longer having to change the globes when alarms went off in the middle of the night.

A timber skeleton-like structure was the first light established at McCrae. It was later taken by bullock wagon to the top of Arthur's Seat to be used as a lookout. The current lighthouse was built in 1874 in England and erected at McCrae in 1883. With a height of 33.5 metres it is the tallest on the Victorian mainland, with a characteristic flash every fifteen seconds and a range of thirteen Nautical Miles. It was used in conjunction with the South Channel Pile Light for channel-centre guidance and was most valuable for ships returning from Geelong.

Phil loves the entire Mornington Peninsula, especially the water. `There couldn't be a better place to live. It is the atmosphere - not country, not city - somewhere in between. The Peninsula has everything´. His favourite beach is McCrae because the water gets deep quickly and there is no need to walk far. `The southern end of the bay is something to be proud of. It is so clean that people always comment in amazement when they can see the sandy bottom´.

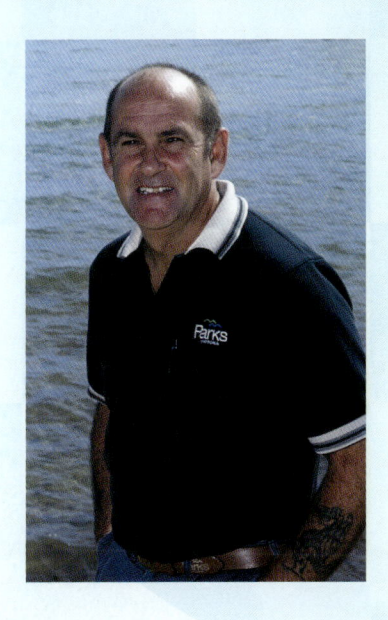

Eastern Lighthouse, McCrae

Pegs Beach, McCrae

beach boxes

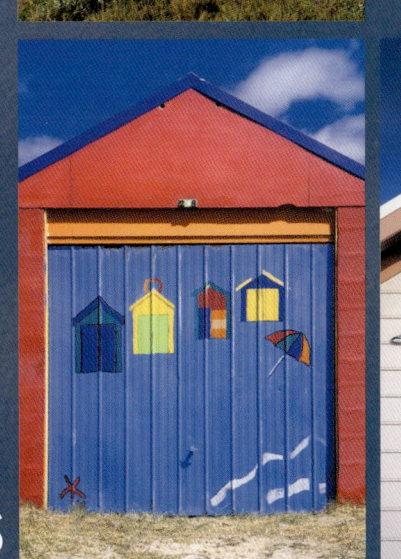

boat sheds

beach huts

bathing boxes

Rosebud

Rosebud was originally a fishing village called Banksia Point. It was a shipwreck that gave the town its official name. The vessel Rosebud was washed ashore in 1855 and a plaque now marks the position on the foreshore.

Rosebud Pier

As idle as a painted ship
Upon a painted ocean
    The Ancient Mariner Part IV

Meet Bridgit Thomas
LOCAL ARTIST

There is a calm and poise about Bridgit that puts one at ease. She has a penchant for painting fish, crabs and seashells as well as etching big ships and sailing boats in Port Phillip Bay. Her studio is a backyard timber shed overlooking Chinamans Creek.

Starfish and crab specimens have accumulated among her pencils and sketchbooks, studied for their finest details. Bridgit's children are accustomed to the `fridge full of smelly fish´. Bridgit is fascinated with the recording of natural history. She prefers to paint her sea creatures when they are freshly caught before their colours fade. Her watercolours are pure and vibrant, shimmering as if still submerged in the sea, like Bridgit herself barefoot and serene wading through water.

Elegant compositions of fish depict a variety of species spatially arranged to compliment the individual shape, size and colour of each. The final artwork is chart-like. Bridgit's Couta boats and big ships are pristine, inclusive of the finest detail and meticulously drawn to scale.

While her artwork adorns the walls of media personalities like Steve Vizard and Rex Hunt, Bridgit treasures her time-out. She loves the quiet candle-lit dinners with family and friends in her private beach box on the foreshore that she shares with kookaburras. Ships slip by, never unnoticed.

Meet Bill Page

ROSEBUD RESIDENT

Bill Page first came to Rosebud in 1945. He moors his dinghy in front of the Motorboat Squadron, a harbour for small boats west of Rosebud pier. Bill identifies his fishing boat by the onion bags hung to deter birds. He recounts the time when the tides were much higher and the car park was under water. `There were no trees here as there are today and water came in a lot further. It is necessary to dredge the small harbour because the sands are shifting. Even the pier has been relocated twice because it became land-bound. In the early days the paddle steamers passed us by and Rosebud was slow to develop´.

Bill loves to watch the big ships turn sharply at the Hovell Pile. `Because the shipping lane is close to the shore at that point, ship spotters are never disappointed. It often seems that the vessels are headed straight for the pier and up the main street´.

Rosebud Harbour

ROSEBUD

Rosebud Harbour and Arthurs Seat

Meet Dennis Chryssikos
ROSEBUD FISHERMAN

Dennis is one of those anonymous characters who regularly fishes at the end of the Rosebud pier. His favourite catch is squid and he willingly shares his traditional Greek recipe to anyone who is interested. Dressed to withstand the rain, offshore winds and sea spray from the wake of passing ships, Dennis appreciates the solitude. He knows the seasons, the types of fish and loves this special spot.

`Good people live here - never have any trouble. All fishermen talk with each other but never ask too many questions´.

Rosebud Pier

Meet Malcolm Brown
FORESHORE RANGER/MANAGER

Who rides a bicycle at work? Malcolm Brown. He is the foreshore ranger who manages the four kilometres of foreshore from Chinaman's Creek to Rye. Malcolm thinks the campers are terrific. `It's only day trippers that pose problems´. When asked how many of the 320 campsites are rebooked for the following year, Malcolm replies, `320´. He works for the Capel Sound Foreshore Committee under the guidance of government coastal strategies. This foreshore is self-funded by revenues generated from campers, ninety-two boat sheds and the boat ramp at Tootgarook.

Malcolm's role is diverse. He undertakes many duties including administration, staff employment, track maintenance, weed control and re-vegetation programs. The peak time for the campers is Boxing Day to mid-January when Malcolm describes the experience as `unbelievable!´ His main clients are families from the eastern suburbs who book the same sites a year in advance. `People remember their beach holidays for a long time and I try to ensure that those memories are always good´. In looking after this foreshore for the community Malcolm strives to attain the vital balance between conservation goals and public enjoyment.

Tootgarook

Tootgarook was a grazing area in the 1800's and the name is thought to mean `land of the croaking frogs´. It has a sandy, gently sloping beach with low-grassed sand dunes and Banksias. When the tide is out there are many exposed sandbanks giving the beach a distinctive character. The small boat ramp attracts pelicans that wait for fishermen to clean their catch.

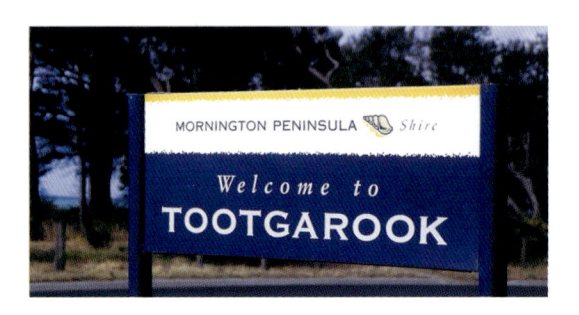

TOOTGAROOK

'The Island'

Rye

Rye was originally called *Whitecliffs* and it remains the name given to the quieter western area of the town. Limeburners were the first permanent settlers during the 1840's and a kiln still exists at the base of the prominent headland. The pier was built in 1860 to transport the lime to Melbourne from the fourteen kilns in Rye. Lime was traditionally used by the building industry as a masonry mortar for structural walls and ornamental plaster.

Rye is the first bayside town on the Peninsula to offer a front and back beach. The bay beach has a long stretch of shallow water loved particularly by windsurfers, whereas the rough ocean beach is popular with surfers and fishermen. This family seaside resort has a continental feel and carnival atmosphere.

Crystal clear sea

The Octopuses Garden at the Rye pier is the first underwater marine trail in Victoria.

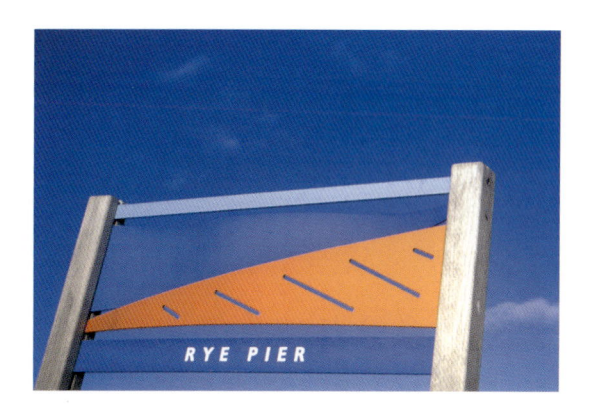

Sand sculpting

Sculpturing sand is a world-class event on the Rye foreshore during summer. About 1500 tonnes of sand (110 truck loads) are used to make huge sand sculptures. Initial preparation requires sand and water to be pounded into formwork timber frames. As the sand is compacted, it stabilises and dries. Carving starts from the top. Once finished the formwork below is removed and the next level down is revealed continuing the process to the ground.

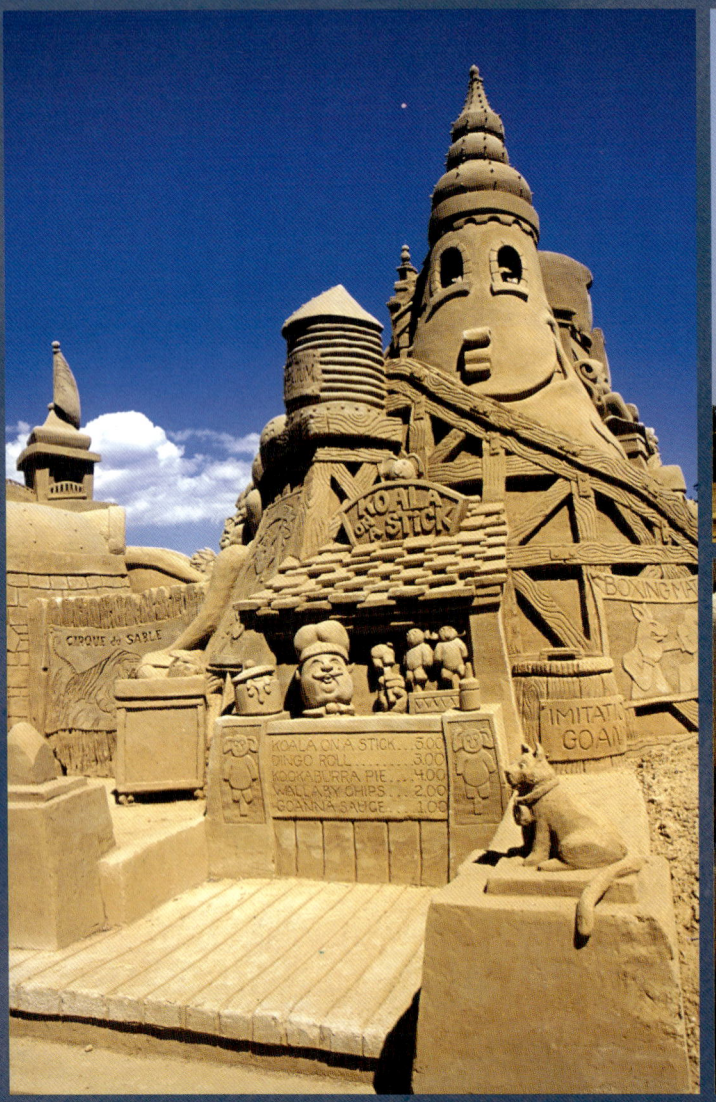

Beach boxes, Tyrone Foreshore

Meet Katie Parkes
WHITECLIFFS, RYE

Katie Parkes leaves Melbourne each week to relax in her `Rye Opera House´ at Whitecliffs. This spectacular multi-level timber home is one of the best known on the Port Phillip coastline and has been the subject of significant media coverage. When not strolling along the Rye foreshore with Baylie, her Bernese Mountain-dog, Katie relishes the spectacular bay view from the balcony or works in her nouveau office extension. Katie equates this to her `tree-house´.

With a wicked laugh, friendly disposition and a philosophical view on life, Katie ponders, `Where would you rather be? I just surrender to my belief that the universe has the plan. How lucky I am. There will not be a FOR SALE sign here!´

Katie's Guest Book reads: `What a beautiful vase for a tall poppy´.

The white quadripod covering a metallic geodetic mark was used as a navigation aid prior to radar. They exist at various points along the bay. The structure was destroyed in 2002 and replaced by the modern black trig marker. A trig station is used as a tool in map making and surveying. It is usually placed at the highest point of the terrain or on the extremities of a land mass.

Navigational marker, Whitecliffs

Trig Station, Whitecliffs

Rye Pier

South from Whitecliffs

Striking silhouette of Moonahs

Blairgowrie

The road sign reads `Village by the Bay´ and the small strip of shops provides the clue to its special character. Friendly retailers provide essentials while cafes provide water bowls for canine customers. It is a family beach loved by locals and visitors seeking a quiet alternative.

The Blairgowrie Safe Boat Harbour opened in 2002 providing floating marina berths for 170 boats and a public mooring area for up to forty-five visiting craft. It is a safe haven for vessels in distress and ready access for rescue craft. The mooring area is protected by a wave attenuator screen that does not extend to the seabed therefore it permits natural water movement. The Blairgowrie Yacht Squadron is recognized as being a magnificent host venue for sailing championships.

Blairgowrie Safe Boat Harbour

Blairgowrie Café

Blairgowrie Yacht Squadron

Groynes are fence-like structures usually made of timber or rock which are built across a beach and into the water. Where waves arrive at right angles to the shore, a series of groynes can trap sand and build small beaches between them to preserve the foreshore.

Blairgowrie to Arthurs Seat

Hutchins Jetty

Camerons Bight was named after the kiln operator who occupied a hut on the foreshore in the 1850s. The Camerons Bight Boat Club was formed in 1974 to acquire the Hutchins family jetty which was rebuilt by club members in 1979. Five generations of the Hutchins family have centred their fishing activities there since 1895. This jetty is situated at the site of the first European landing and settlement in Victoria in 1803.

BLAIRGOWRIE

Winter fog

Sorrento

The foreshore in front of the town is one of the most interesting and picturesque esplanades on the Peninsula. It still retains a promenade essence with its century old bandstand. The vision and energy of George Selth Coppin (1819-1906) created the perfect seaside resort. His paddle-steamer company brought tourists to Sorrento and a steam tram transported them from the front pier to the back beach. Rotundas, walkways and lookouts were provided for their enjoyment. Locally quarried limestone was used to build guesthouses, hotels and public buildings.

Sorrento still has a special charm that ensures visitors keep returning. Ocean Beach Road contains elegant eateries, boutiques, galleries and specialist shops. Sorrento's main street connects the calm front beach - a foreshore framed by Norfolk pines silhouetting against Port Phillip Bay - to the rough ocean beach on Bass Strait.

Coppins Jetty and Sorrento township

Ferry Terminal

Sorrento Foreshore

With the demise of summer, the town seemed to settle down on itself, to mellow. The breeze no longer carried the crackle of transistors, the call of gulls and the smell of fish and chips. With the summer visitors gone, there was a sense of quiet industry about the place. It was the business of getting on with things.

From HOTEL SORRENTO by Hannie Rayson.

Coppins Jetty

George Coppins' Company built the swimming baths at Coppins Jetty in 1875. It was `secured by a fence to exclude large fish…a red flag denotes gentlemen's hours: a white flag for ladies´.

Sorrento Foreshore

SORRENTO

Coppins Jetty

`Each sunrise gives hope to your dreams and light to your plans´.
WILLIAM NGWAKA MAPHOTO

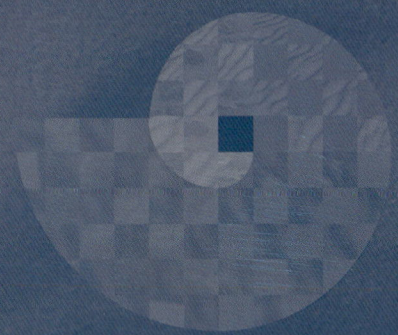

Many warm-toned nineteenth century limestone buildings contribute to Sorrento's romantic heritage character.

St John's Anglican Church is classified by the National Trust. The neo-Gothic nave was completed in 1875.

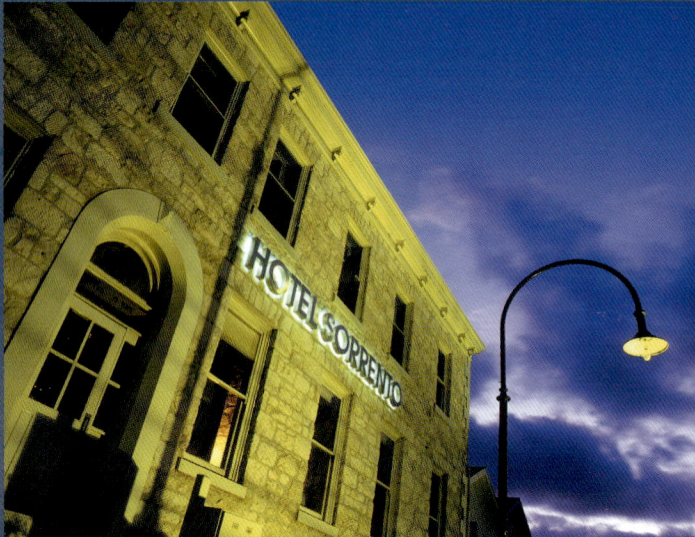

Hotel Sorrento was built by John Farnsworth in 1872. It is the oldest commercial building in the town.

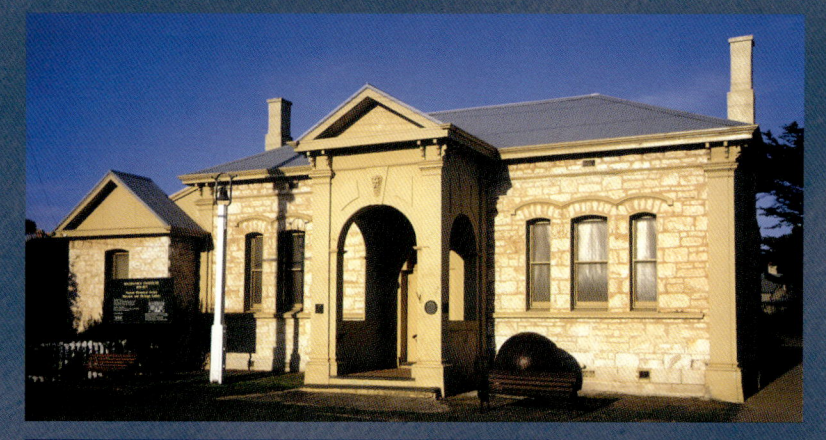

The Mechanics' Institute (1876) was the heart of activities in the town, being used as a library, entertainment venue, law court, Red Cross Centre through two World Wars and now the Nepean Historical Society.

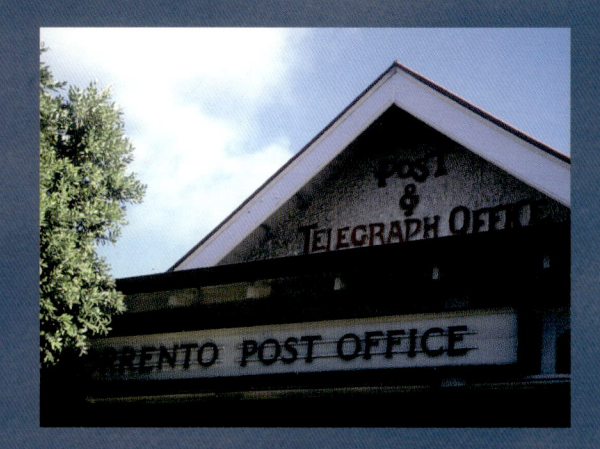

(Circa 1905-6)

(Circa 1890)

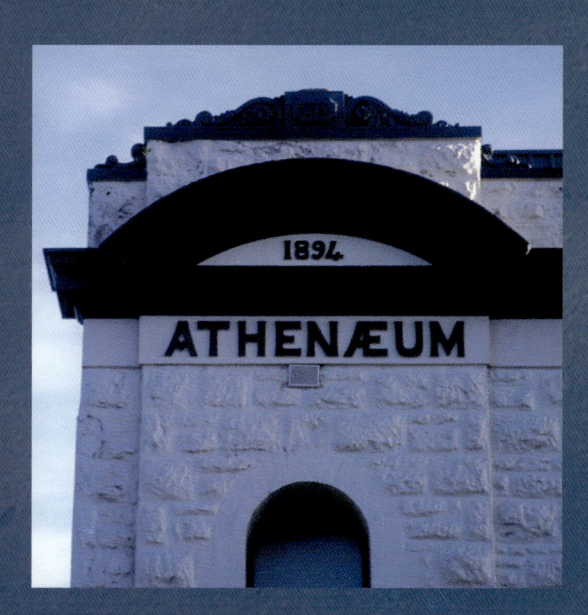

The Athenaeum Theatre was built in 1894 as a concert hall and ballroom. Its current cinema function had beginnings in the early 1900's when the theatre became the venue for silent picture shows.

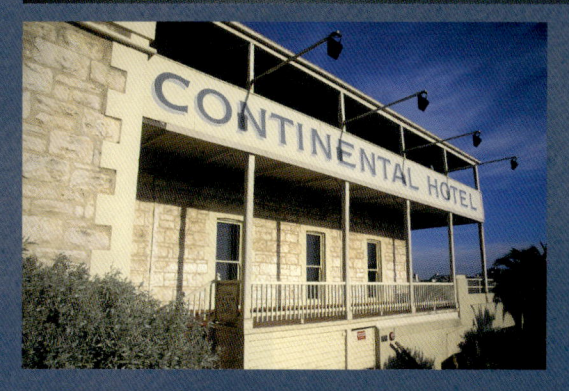

The Continental Hotel, referred to as 'the Contie', is said to be the tallest limestone building in Victoria. It dates from 1875 and was built by Coppins' Ocean Ampitheatre Company.

77

Meet Tim Phillips

WOODEN BOAT SHOP

Tim Phillips loves `a boat that smiles´. Thanks to dedicated craftsmen the traditional art of wooden boat building has survived the turn of another century. The Wooden Boat Shop in Sorrento has played a vital role in keeping the magic of Couta boats alive. Its principal objective is `the revival, restoration and preservation of Australian Couta boats and their heritage´.

Victoria has the largest Couta boat fleet in the world with the majority in Sorrento. Today they are used for social sailing, racing, cruising and recreational fishing. Couta boats are typically 26' open sailing boats with a 3' 3" draft. They are gaff-rigged with a wide cockpit area originally used for fish storage - now it is not unusual to accommodate a crew of eight to ten on board. A rig peculiar to the Victorian Couta boats evolved which allowed the sail to be carried higher than usual including a distinctive curved-down bowsprit.

The Couta boats had their origins in the needs of hard-working fishermen. The target fish was *barracouta* (hence the name). These large fish were the mainstay of the `fish and chip´ trade supply in Melbourne, but in the 1880's demand could not be satisfied within the bay. A design evolved to enable fishing outside the treacherous Rip where their qualities of sea worthiness were proven. When each boat had reached its fishing quota it would race back to port as fast as possible in order to secure the best market price for the catch. While load carrying capacity was important the need for speed was also vital. Couta boats continued to be used as commercial fishing vessels until the 1950's when they were phased out as a result of improvement in engine technology and a growing preference for shark in the market.

Unfortunately the art of wooden-boat building is disappearing. Tim Phillips with his team of specialist craftsmen and a small band of enthusiasts has worked to ensure these boats sail forever. Not only does Tim build and restore Couta boats, he is heavily involved in conducting Couta boat events from the Sorrento Sailing Couta Boat Club.

Tim learned the trade from original masters including the late Ken Lacco whose name is synonymous with Couta boats. All the work is done by hand using traditional methods. `Ken Lacco was my inspiration. He is the father figure to what has happened here. Ken taught me to build, then told me to design. He took the baton from his father Mitch Lacco, then passed it - not only passed it, but also parcelled it up to hand to me. I want to do the same´.

`People like Ken make Australia great´. Ken Lacco passed away in 2002. His boats came to life. His superb wooden boats have economy of line and superior sea-keeping qualities. Fast, efficient and beautiful. `In the world of fishing craft there was no equal but he represented more than that. He was a passionate man, a lover of fine things, possessing extraordinary powers of observation and intelligence. In another life he would have achieved lots of other great things´.

Couta Boats

Meet Andrew Mackinnon

THIRD GENERATION SORRENTO

The Mackinnon family. Locals know the name. Old Sorrento. Andrew is the third generation descendant from this fishing family. In 1911 his grandfather Charles moved to Sorrento. He later purchased *Mermerus*, a Couta boat built in 1936 by the legendary Ken Lacco.

Andrew Mackinnon was virtually raised on a Couta boat in an era of fishermen. It was the only life he knew. Asked to reflect upon his childhood days in Sorrento, `I had no say in it. I happened to be born here´.

`My childhood seemed commonplace at the time. As a ten year old I went with Dad, my grandfather and others to the rocket practice day held once a month on a Saturday afternoon. It was a forerunner to the rescue squad as there were no lifeboats at the ocean beaches. The purpose was to check equipment and practice the routine for launching a rescue line to ships in trouble´.

`The men used me as their breeches boy. An elaborate system of blocks and poles was concreted into the rocks at London Bridge and Pearses Beach. I had to sit in the life-ring that looked like a pair of bloomers, then hang-on while I was transferred from one side of the practice area to the other. If it were an actual rescue, a rocket would launch the line and blocks would be set up on the boat´.

An amalgam of memories from that bygone era helps explain the man in his forties. Andrew has been described as a loner, somewhat elusive. He mirrors his father's shyness, cautious of new friendship and stubborn. Few who know him well say Andrew is a chatty, fun-loving guy - caring and good. He maintains `they gave up teaching common sense when I left school´.

Andrew's property resembles a nautical museum with boats and cars, timber and bluestone bricks alongside his father's possessions. He bought bollards from the old Port Melbourne jetty and timbers from South Wharf. His bedposts are red gum piles from the old Sorrento Baths.

His hobbies? For more than twenty years Andrew has photographed ships and knows the name and origin of every vessel entering the bay. Andrew shares the ships with anyone who is interested and sends his photos to shipping societies around the world.

Launching ramp

SORRENTO

Winter fog

Along this section of the Sorrento coastline land ownership extends to the high water mark making access along the water's edge difficult. The cliff face is privately owned as are the jetties and `bathing boxes on water´.

Private jetties with beach boxes are unique to Sorrento and Portsea. Some have retained the swimming enclosures which were constructed to provide protection from sharks. The cliff face is decorated with a network of wooden walkways connecting the cliff top home with its private jetty. It is interesting to identify which jetty is attached to each property because many are coordinated with colour or decorative features.

The scenic walk through private cliff top properties, from Lentell Avenue to Point King, is not sign posted. A high, uninviting green gate is the starting point. The pathway follows an old right of way (500metres long) on `land granted in 1910 to King George V, his heirs and successors, for public use and convenience´.

`Are we walking through someone's property?´

Cliff top walk from Sorrento to Portsea

Point King to Point McArthur. At Point King there is a stone cairn and symbolic flagpole commemorating the cliff top where Lieutenant John Murray raised the Union Jack in 1802. Artists paint from this high point to capture the views of bathing boxes and jetties below.

Point King Beach, Portsea

Meet Cathie Maney

ARTIST/DESIGNER

CATHIE MANEY is well known worldwide for her colourful artwork of boatsheds, fish and dolphins. Paintings, plates and vases are displayed in her Portsea gallery while her bed linen and bathroom accessories can be purchased in stores.

It was the threat of demolishing the Point King boatsheds that inspired Cathie's first painting. `They were the really quirky things about the area - the source of its character´. Cathie has lived in Sorrento, Gunnamatta and Portsea. She needs to move in order to recreate her design work. Cathie loves Portsea. She feels free and safe and adores the outdoors. It's perfect for her young family. Cathie loves to paint. Her paintings are the gift of freedom - to do what she wants - to create. `This area has been fantastic to me. There is something special down here, though I cannot define what it is´.

Cathie tries to explain the significant lapses between her paintings. She believes `it is important at times for everyone to pull back and slow down. It's hard to do, but you risk losing yourself, your very essence. The whole world needs to´. She is always looking for that special `thing´ which sparks direction, but also warns that the more you push, the less it will come to you. Cathie Maney is talented and successful, friendly and warm. She appreciates life and exudes contentment.

Point King

PORTSEA

Weeroona Bay

Meet Ross McColl

SHELLEY BEACH - FOURTH GENERATION

Shelley beach is Ross McColl's home and he considers himself a local. `I live here and go to Melbourne to work. We come down every Friday evening, have dinner at a local restaurant, drive to Melbourne for school sport Saturday morning then return until Sunday night´.

In the 1890's Ross' great-grandfather bought the strip of land extending from the existing car park on the cliff top down to the flat section of beach. He built his retreat at the top. The lime kiln, which was operated by the Skeltons still exists on the land next door. Ross' childhood memories then began.

`We had a Seagull outboard moored inside the blue line and Grandma would ring her bell from the cliff top to call us for lunch. When she knew someone aboard a passing ship she would hang white sheets on the washing line to convey her farewell wave. Plum puddings in muslin bags were hung on that same line. She was memorable. When we got soil from Red Hill to make her hydrangeas purple, Grandma would help wheel in the barrow loads´.

Ross' grandfather built the boat shed on the foreshore, complete with limestone chimney. It was equipped with a Coolgardie Safe and kerosene lanterns. His father recounted times when the water lapped at the door during high tides. The beach has increased in recent years as the bay has silted up significantly and moorings have been relocated out of necessity.

Many changes have occurred. Locals used to shop in Portsea regularly. There was a butcher's store, Stringer's groceries, milk bar, newsagents, post office, two pubs and home deliveries of milk, bread and newspapers. Now it is difficult to attribute an identity to the town centre. Galleries, real estate agents and diving schools proliferate.

Few properties still consist of both the flat land on the beach as well as the top section. When property was bequeathed among family members subdivision effectively occurred and the introduction of land tax was prohibitive for many of the original landowners.

`Our new home has been built at the site where my grandfather tended his vegetables as he looked out to sea. It is what he wanted. Many times as a child he would point to that patch and hope our name would remain at Shelley Beach forever´.

PORTSEA

Bathing box at sea

Private jetty with bathing box and swimming enclosure at Shelley Beach

I am Delgany
The castle on the hill
Built in the 1920's by Harold Armytage
Whose ghost walks within me still
When the moon is full, he stands aloft
And from my turrets he surveys
His beautiful gardens, his majestic trees
That hauntingly whisper as they sway
In a gentle breeze
Long shadows fall across the lawns
There is a warmth flowing through
This ghostly form
For his dream of Delgany has been reborn.

- PATRICIA APPLEFORD
FIRST VERSE

Delgany

Agapanthas are prolific in this coastal town and are often referred to as Portsea Roses.

Delgany was built in the 1920's as a private home and modelled on a Scottish castle. The history of the mansion is tinged with sorrow. It was Harold Armytage's dream to create a fairytale castle and he spared no expense in acquiring the limestone from Mt Gambier. Tragically he died before he was able to move in. Delgany was used as a war hospital and in 1948 was the first school in Victoria for deaf children. Since 1988 Delgany has been a seaside retreat in Portsea.

Meet Stephen Eastop
CHIEF EXECUTIVE OFFICER, PORTSEA CAMP

Surely there is nothing more important to our future as a nation, than our children?
- Dame Beryl Beaurepaire, AC, DBE, OBE, Patron of The Portsea Camp

Since 1945 the Portsea camp has provided a wonderful environment for children of Victoria with a major focus on those who are disadvantaged and have special needs. It occupies the site of fortifications built in 1889 when gun emplacements, a fort and barracks were constructed. During the Second World War Fort Franklin was used as an army base and hospice. It is now owned and run by the Board of Trustees, a charitable organization.

`This is our sea change´, explains Stephen Eastop. He lives on site with his wife Sabra and son Liam. `Life here is hectic seven days a week. With three hundred people on our doorstep there is little privacy. We inherited a backlog of poor maintenance and old equipment so it was a huge task. It was surreal in the beginning - an oversized caravan park with people knocking on the door with questions we couldn't answer and problems we couldn't solve!´

Stephen has a professional outlook. `We are responsible for children twenty-four hours a day and sacrifice a lot to do this properly. It is a big personal challenge but it is possible to make a significant difference. We are addressing inequality in an area of inequity. Affecting how people feel when they are here is more important than beds, food and big swings´.

`Many of the kids here have had a hard time. If a kid has failed at school, at home or with friends we provide the chance to meet new kids and adults and experience being where they are valued. We show by example that there are better ways to treat people´.

Stephen says the area makes him `feel he is on holidays even when he is not. And we have learned so much about the weather because we are surrounded by it. The sea is our backyard and I would rather be in a storm here, than anywhere else´.

Sabra is also very philosophic. She has learned it is possible to make significant changes and the only obstacle in her way is herself. Lack of privacy is the main struggle. `It is impossible being the Brady Bunch all the time! We are old travellers who love secluded places and need to escape at times in order to cope. It is important to step back for our privacy and we greatly appreciate the buffer of people's consideration´.

The annual Portsea Swim Classic is one of the largest open water swims held in Australia. This L-shaped course covers 1.2km and attracts around 2000 swimmers.

Point Nepean

Point Nepean is a thin strip of land at the tip of the Mornington Peninsula. It has the cold, volatile waters of Bass Strait on one side and the calmer, warm waters of Port Phillip Bay on the other. For more than a century it was closed to the public. Point Nepean has been a place of isolation - set apart by topography and its historical functions of quarantine and defence.

The series of fortifications built above and below ground at Fort Nepean demonstrate the importance attached to protecting Victoria against seaborne invasion in the 1880's.

Marine National Parks are designated areas in the bay where over 1000 species of plant and animals and 500 species of fish are fully protected. Swimmers, sailors, divers, snorkellers and bird-watchers are able to observe an abundance of amazing marine life, including dolphins and seals. *Port Phillip Heads Marine National Park* includes Mud Island, Popes Eye, Point Nepean, Portsea Hole, Point Lonsdale and Swan Bay.

The Rip

The Rip

The narrow entrance to Port Phillip Bay is called The Rip. It is 2.7 kilometres wide, half of which is reef locked with a navigable stretch of only 700 metres. The narrowness and the depth of over ninety metres create havoc for vessels. There is turmoil on the surface as the incoming five to seven knot tide surges into the bay meeting the outgoing tide. The Rip is one of the most hazardous stretches of water in the world. Nearly 100 ships have foundered and many lives have been lost. Ships entering or leaving the bay must carry a pilot unless the skipper is one of the fifteen per cent who has an `exemption certificate´.

When an incoming vessel requires a pilot, radio contact is made with the service. A powerful launch is used to convey the pilot several kilometres outside the Heads. He boards the ship by climbing a rope ladder that has been slung over the side, enters the bridge and takes control until docking at Melbourne or Geelong. It is dramatic to observe the pilot as he leaves the orange launch. The speed of both vessels must be coordinated perfectly and calculated in accordance with the size of the waves and the powerful tides.

The Rip is located between Point Nepean and Point Lonsdale. The Point Lonsdale lighthouse is still manned 24 hours a day.

Meet Captain Peter Seal and Captain Geoffrey Beevers

PORT PHILLIP SEA PILOTS

The Port Phillip Pilots Service is a private organization that has operated since 1838 from Queenscliff. It has a long and proud history. The 32 sea pilots were all former ships' captains and some are third generation pilots. They guide 5000 ships per annum working 24-hour rosters, seven days a week throughout the entire year. Despite the sophistication of navigational equipment, the safe movement of ships is dependent on the experience and agility of the pilots.

Captain Peter Seal has been in the Pilots Service for twenty-seven years. His great, great grandfather was a sea pilot. He concedes that the job is hazardous not only at night or during storms. The underwater trench in The Rip is approximately 93 metres deep, like Niagara Falls under the sea. Even on calm days the seas boil and the water is unforgiving. A dangerous mix of flood and ebb tides create whirlpools on the surface.

Captain Seal explained that radar is used as well as the Black and White lighthouses at Queenscliff in order to align vessels with the centre of the 245-metre wide Great Ship Channel. `But it is not what you do, it's how you do it´, he says. `Familiarity with the territory is crucial. If you run off the road in the Bay, you won't get back. There are forces out there you cannot see on the radar and they need to be anticipated before they occur, with no room for error´.

Captain Geoffrey Beevers, a seapilot for twenty years, has confronted the dangers, embraced personal challenge and shared many anecdotes. `I liken the exhilaration of my job with that of achieving excellence in a dangerous sport. A seapilot operates in a high-risk environment and must utilize skill and experience to neutralize the risk of taking an ocean-going ship close to dangers of the shore and dangers under the sea. Very few jobs offer comparable satisfaction´.

Pilot boarding a container ship

Captain Peter Seal

Captain Geoffrey Beevers

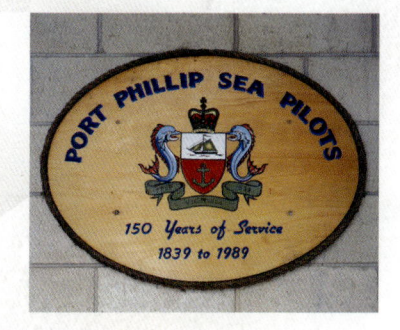

Tugs are usually required to assist vessels within the restricted boundaries of a port to turn around and to facilitate the berthing process. Eight tugs operate from Port Phillip Bay.

We cannot direct the wind but we can adjust the sails.
ANONYMOUS

Pilot launch

Cargo ship entering Port Phillip Bay through the Rip

Point Lonsdale Pier, the Rip and Point Nepean

Portsea Surf Beach

Portsea Surf Lifesaving Club patrols the dangerous ocean beach over summer. Red and yellow flags indicate the safe swimming area and the blue flags are positioned for board riders inside the Surf-Craft Area.

Rescue Tube. The swimmer in distress grasps the tube or it is clipped around his body and towed to safety. This device is used close to shore.

Inflatable Rescue Boat. The IRB or `Rubber Ducky´ is the fastest and most manoeuvrable piece of lifesaving equipment which is able to perform a rescue of multiple patients.

Meet Will Dwyer and Felicity Milford

PORTSEA LIFESAVERS

Lifeguards are trained to keep the beaches safe. Will Dwyer has been an active member of the Portsea Surf Lifesaving Club since he was fifteen and is now a paid patrol captain during summer. His training qualifications include a Silver Medallion, Senior First Aid Certificate and Advanced Resuscitation Certificate. Prior to starting any patrol, he will survey the area to identify the safest swimming environment and potential hazards both in and out of the water. This will determine where warning signs, rescue equipment and flags are placed. He delegates specific roles to the lifesavers on duty.

`One of the dangers is getting washed sideways ending up in a current and being taken out to sea. We have to ensure that swimmers keep between the red and yellow flags´. Will acknowledges that Portsea back beach is very dangerous with strong rips and currents. `Members here have excellent surf awareness. If you can swim here, you can swim anywhere´.

Felicity Milford is a volunteer lifesaver working weekends and holidays until Easter. `Each year we need to complete a proficiency test to ensure our fitness levels are suitable and our expertise with the equipment is up to date. It is a big responsibility´. Over summer Felicity loves living at the Club which accommodates up to sixty members. `Everyone loves having dinner on the deck at sunset seeing London Bridge and Sphinx Rock in the distance´.

Portsea Surf Lifesaving Club

Meet Kim de Heer

COPPIN'S TEAROOM AND KIOSK

Kim and Ken de Heer opened Coppins in December 1995. Their original plan had only included a kiosk and a summer commitment. It was sparked by their holidays on the Mornington Peninsula and their eventual move to Blairgowrie. Business started in the carpark with a caravan selling hotdogs and donuts over three summers. Now they operate the tearoom and a kiosk all year around.

Kim modestly attributes the success of their restaurant to the magnificent views of Bass Strait. `It is a perfect location from which to experience the ocean's changing moods aware that Antarctica lies in a wilderness beyond the horizon´. Kim loves to observe that instant when people experience the panorama for the first time. The visitors' book contains entries from celebrities and world travellers who love the unique location and greatly appreciate Kim's warmth and hospitality.

Coppins is popular with visitors all year round. It is frenetic in summer, relaxing in spring and autumn. Winter is the time when the locals venture out, safe from the tourist crowds. Ken loves the seasons. When he is not at the tearooms he is involved in major projects at the Surf Lifesaving Club. Ken maintains, `The Coppins Track along the cliff top is world class - better than Capri - each cove and bay is different. If the track was concreted we would have more visitors than the Great Ocean Road´.

The boardwalk from Coppin's Lookout

SORRENTO OCEAN BEACH

The Amphitheatre

This section of ocean beach between Coppins Lookout and Pulpit Rock was promoted in the late 1890's as `a picturesque crescent of rocks and sand offering elevated views of the ocean´. The geographical features resemble the rising gallery in a theatre, hence its name.

Many young surfers hang out to develop their skills on this shore break. `This place is best when it's at its worst. When the wind is blowing dead on shore and the tide is mid to high, you can have a ball out there. It doesn't matter where you surf as long as you enjoy it!´ Ted Bainbridge, Peninsula Surf Centre.

Darby Rock. The rock-stack offshore was once part of the mainland having resisted erosion better than the surrounding rock. It is possible to walk out to Darby Rock at low tide. According to local legend it was named after a fisherman called Darbyshire who was caught by a king-tide and stranded there for several days.

A rockpool at low tide reflects Coppins Lookout.

SORRENTO OCEAN BEACH

Coppins Lookout was officially opened in 1970. It was built on the site of an original rotunda constructed in the 1870's. Two brass plaques - line of sight directions - indicate the direction and distance of sixty locations to the north, east and west. `Melbourne-37 miles. Flinders-19 miles. Hobart-340 miles. Mud Islands-5 miles´. Yachtsmen sailing Bass Strait appreciate that it is one of the few identifiable landmarks on the Mornington Peninsula coastline.

The large rock pool exposed at low tide is a Sorrento icon. During summer children queue to take turns at jumping into the transparent blue water. Concrete edging constructed in the 1930's has nearly disintegrated.

Lifeguards on duty, Sorrento Ocean Beach

Bay of Islands. Coast cliffs are receding as they are attacked and undermined by storm waves. The process is more rapid when the shore platform is narrow or absent.

Montforts Beach

BLAIRGOWRIE

One can make a day of any size,
regulate the rising and setting of his own sun
and the brightness of its shining.
    Anonymous

Sunset at Montforts Beach

The Bridge, Bridgewater Bay

At the eastern end of Bridgewater Bay there is a deep crystal-clear rock pool which is exposed at low tide. The cliff above has three natural landings from which to jump or dive.

Jumping from The Bridge

Meet Neil Briggs

LONG TERM RESIDENT

Blairgowrie in the early 1950's - sand tracks, no services, vacant land and fibro weekenders, tank water, wood stoves and languid summers were Neil's first recollections. He treasures the many weekend trips with his parents where he learned to swim in rockpools at the back beach. He also spent many hours enjoying the low tides on the Blairgowrie foreshore where beach cricket, paddle-boarding and formative sailing techniques were honed.

In 1969, Neil returned to Blairgowrie as a full-time resident to repeat history with his own family. Neil recalls the days when he was undertaking professional qualifications. In order to complete his assignments he sought solitude without disruption at his special hideaways. These places still afford an escape from his busy office and a time to reflect.

By the new millennium Blairgowrie has changed. Nearly every block is built upon and at times the seaside town assumes a lively character. However, the charm and personality endures and Neil's roots are well entrenched. Neil's favourite location is between Pearse's beach and Dimmick's beach at Jessie Kirwoods Rock. It is Neil's *contemplation point*, a place for quiet - a solo sojourn.

`The sea wind removes the stubborn cobwebs and the sea breeze rejuvenates the soul. There is stunning beauty looking east to Cape Schanck and west to Point Nepean - a vista defined by moods of the sea. Salt spray and sea mists from Bass Strait give an eerie appearance. It can be wild and tempestuous, at other times a millpond. Sharks surf on waves´.

`At low tide rock pools appear and access is granted to secluded caves and cliffs. After high tide there is purity of sand. The only footprints are mine. Robinson Crusoe. It is possible to transport yourself to anywhere you desire to be´.

Jessie Kirwoods Rock

BLAIRGOWRIE

Dimmicks Beach

The Divide

The Divide represents a significant indentation into the coastal cliff formation between Dimmicks Beach, Blairgowrie and Number Sixteen Beach, Rye. This landform can be appreciated from the cliff top which is accessed by a track off the main walking path. The cliff is steep and dangerous, the waves powerful and unpredictable, giving the feel of a deserted coastline.

A rock platform pitted with potholes and weathered rock formations is exposed at extremely low tides only. From here it is possible with caution to view The Divide from the shoreline. This access is only possible by walking westward from Number Sixteen Beach.

The Divide, Rye

Number Sixteen Beach

According to Park Rangers, Number Sixteen Beach was named in the `pre street directory days´ when the coast was divided into thirty areas and attributed a number. This enabled rescues to be conducted more efficiently because it was possible to identify the exact location of the swimmers or sailors in distress. The old Life Saving Track (now the Peninsula Coastal Walk) runs along the cliff top parallel to the coast from Portsea to here. Number Sixteen is the sixteenth and last access point to the coast from this track.

Rye Ocean Beach

The Rye Ocean Beach is an open, sandy surf beach within the Mornington Peninsula National Park. It is notorious for its rips and considered unsafe for swimming. The Hoax Coast has been used to describe the Peninsula surf in relation to the west coast, which is regarded as the Surf Coast. `It is an affectionate phrase and we can call it that because we live there and secretly like it, but you can't!´ *Warrick Wynne.*

The decision for surfers is complex. Tide, wind, swell and the structure of the seabed all contribute to the quality of a wave. These variables are continually changing.

Surfers can rely on a surf check from the carpark.

St Andrews Ocean Beach

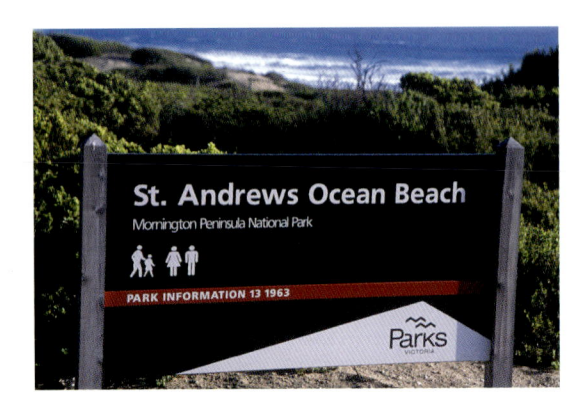

The scale of erosion at St Andrews Ocean Beach gives part of the landward coastal margin a desert-like appearance. There are broad expanses of sand on the beach backed by steep, sparsely vegetated sand dunes.

Horse riding is permitted on St Andrews Beach between Boags Rocks and the beach access track at Paradise Drive. The ride begins along a bush track in single file to the rugged beach where the surf pounds the sand and rock. Horses are permitted to canter along the waves edge but cannot be ridden above the high tide mark or galloped at any time.

Gunnamatta Ocean Beach

The Aboriginal word *Gunnamatta* when translated means `beach and sand hills´. Before the 1960's it was known as Paradise Beach. The shore, seven kilometres long, is considered to be the premier surfing spot for beach break waves on the Mornington Peninsula.

The beach is popular but hazardous. It has sandbars that collapse, submerged rock platforms, deep channels, many rips and an ever-moving ocean floor offshore. Lifesavers find it difficult to find a safe spot for the flags and the gap between them is never great. The beach is fickle and constantly changing.

`The Peninsula Surfriders Club has its home base here and localism can play its part in waves being scarce for visitors´. Richard Loveridge.

The Gunnamatta Life Saving Club with Cape Schanck Lighthouse in the distance.

GUNNAMATTA

Gunnamatta Ocean Beach

Cape Schanck

Cape Schanck is a rugged headland from which lava cliffs protrude southward in an undulating promontory. The ledges of basalt and coves are accessible by a wooden boardwalk out to Pulpit Rock. To the east the rocky cliffs are rimmed with farmland that extends around to Western Port Bay. To the west lies Fingal Beach, which is separated from Cape Schanck by the Selwyn Fault. This is a major displacement of rock structures where the black basalt cliffs on the Cape Schanck side contrast with the softer sands and limestone on the Point Nepean side.

Cape Schanck Lighthouse

Cape Schanck boardwalk

Meet Prue Sheer

LIGHTHOUSE KEEPER

The Cape Schanck Lighthouse was built in 1859 from local limestone. It was the second coastal light established in Victoria, 21 metres high with a range of 40 kilometres. A unique feature is its stone stairway covered with soft lead plating. Each lighthouse has its own sequence of light, in this case the morse-code letter `N´. The main beam is equivalent to 1.6 million candles. Cape Schank Lighthouse is still in operation today guiding many boats along this rugged coastline where scores of ships perished before its construction.

In the late 1800's three lighthouse keepers and their families lived in the lighthouse grounds. The head light keeper had two assistants. Many of the early keepers were former mariners and head keepers were often retired masters of ships. During each watch the keeper had to wind the clockwork, pump kerosene to the burner and generally tend the light. In 1935 electric lamps were installed and these had to be manned day and night until 1987 when a fully automatic system was installed. In 1994 the Australian Maritime Safety Authority established a Differential Global Positioning System (DGPS). This is the tower with wiring and ground grid adjacent to the lighthouse.

Prue Sheer and her husband Tony have been the lighthouse keepers since 1996. They leased the property from Parks Victoria. Prue and Tony manage the kiosk, museum, tours and accommodation in the old lighthouse keepers' cottages. More than 360 000 people visit Cape Schanck annually.

Prue has restored the historic cottages to their original heritage condition and incorporated modern comforts. `I love Victorian history and our guests appreciate the chance to experience this bygone era. People display such passion and feeling for the lighthouse. It is undeniably romantic. The yachtees in particular radiate such warmth and shed an occasional tear. Even though their modern vessels are outfitted with sophisticated navigation aids they hail the visual comfort of the lighthouse at night´.

CAPE SCHANCK

Fragile rock structure eroded by wind and water.

Hinterland

Greens Bush is the largest remnant of bushland on the Peninsula. Surrounded by farmland, this island of native forest is a wildlife haven. Eucalypt forest, banksias and fern gullies are mixed with spectacular strands of grasstree.

Greens Bush

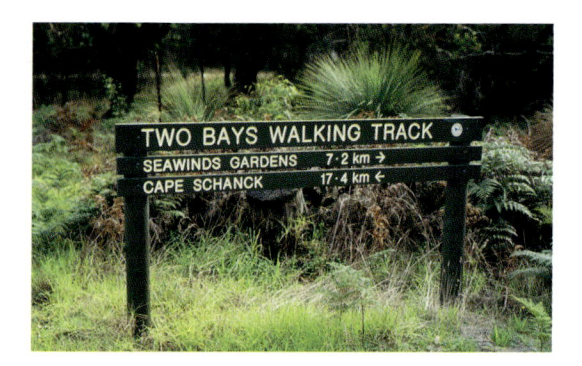

The Two Bays Walking Track is around 30 kilometres in length linking Dromana and Cape Schanck. Large sections of the walk wind through Arthurs Seat State Park and the Greens Bush area of Mornington Peninsula National Park.

At dusk, Eastern Grey kangaroos graze at Highfields Park.

The Mornington Peninsula is now established as one of Australia's great wine regions with more than 170 vineyards and over 50 cellar doors. Montalto Vineyard and Olive Grove is one of the newest. It produces three classic cool climate wines - Pinot Noir, Chardonnay and Riesling. The spectacular property is typical of the Peninsula's rolling green countryside and ocean backdrop.

Red Hill Estate

Montalto vineyard restaurant, Shoreham

Ten Minutes by Tractor Wine Company, Main Ridge

Stoniers Winery, Merricks

Fingal is magnificent dune country renowned for picturesque grazing land and world-class golf courses.

Hinterland

Among the many hinterland attractions are museums, art and craft markets, antique centres, mazes, potteries, historical homesteads, fresh produce farms, galleries and tearooms.

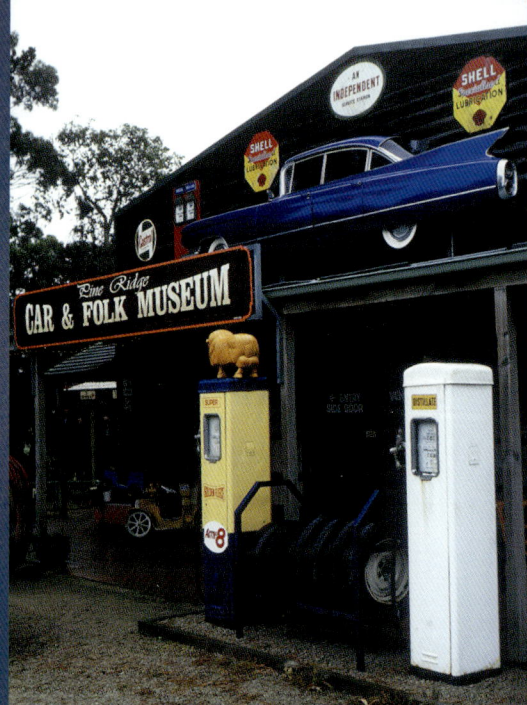

Ashcombe Maze, Shoreham is the oldest hedge maze in Australia. The dense sculptured walls of the hedge structures are two metres wide and three metres in height. Maze Keeper, Arthur Ross maintains the greatest thing about working with nature is seeing the results.

Nobbies View Plant Farm, Shoreham commands a view of Western Port Bay, Phillip Island and the Nobbies. All the plants are grown at the farm without protection from the harsh climatic conditions resulting in very tough, reliable and drought resistant plants.

Kniphofias or Pokers

Watsonias

Grazing land, Flinders

Flinders

Flinders is a nineteenth century fishing village around the corner from the spectacular coastline of Bass Strait. It represents the start of Western Port Bay. The Mornington Peninsula's serene `coast of coves´ extends from Flinders to Somers. Towns here do not attract the huge crowds of Port Phillip Bay. A purity of lifestyle exists with a mix of seaside living and rural pleasures.

Meet Eric Lucas

LIFE MEMBER FLINDERS GOLF CLUB

Putter in hand Eric Lucas crouches over the golf ball. With a strong smooth stroke the ball starts towards the hole. Behind him the waves are completing their journey across Bass Strait. Regarded as one of the most scenic golf courses in Australia, Flinders Golf Course follows the cliff around the coastline with spectacular views from every hole.

Flinders Golf Club celebrated its centenary in 2003. It was founded by prominent members of the Royal Melbourne Golf Club, principally the club champion, David Myles Maxwell. Appropriately Maxwell was originally from the home of golf, St Andrews in Scotland.

Eric Lucas started playing golf when he was eight and only stopped during the war years when he served in the navy. He is the third generation in a family of fishermen at Flinders. Eric's grandfather settled there in the 1890's living in a fisherman's cottage on the foreshore. Crayfish was the main catch. Eric recalls his father's advice. `Respect the sea, watch its every mood and fit in with the changes in weather. If you get into trouble then do one thing at a time, don't change your mind and think positive all the time´. Eric carries these philosophies onto the golf course and through life in general.

A feature of his 68 years membership has been his involvement in coaching young golfers especially with putting. He received an Australian Sports Medal for his contribution to junior golf. It was no surprise when Eric Lucas' putt went straight into the middle of the hole.

Photo courtesy Flinders Golf Club. The third hole *Niagara* was played from the top of the cliff to a green on the edge of the beach. The golfer (left) is David Myles Maxwell, founder of Flinders Golf Course.

Point Leo

Point Leo is nestled into the rural surroundings on Western Port Bay. It was the interest in surfing following the 1956 Olympics that led to the growth of the area. Point Leo started as a remote location for early Malibu (long board) riders and from the 1960's grew as Melbourne's closest surf beach.

The surf beach offers some good point and reef breaks during late autumn through to spring. It is best surfed on an incoming tide. Rips are rare and waves average 0.5 metres. Locals refer to the popular surf breaks as Crunchy, Suicide, Sometimes, First or Second. The back beach is where the East Creek meets the sea and it is an attractive safe swimming area for children.

The gatehouse. An entry fee to the coastal reserve is levied over summer.

'The tide is the music. The wave is the dance'.
The menu board offers daily quotes.

East Creek

Ramp at Point Leo Boat Club

Meet Prue Latchford

EAST COAST SURF SCHOOL

`There is no need to sit and daydream about what it must feel like to surf like experts. If you can swim, you can surf! All you need is a sense of fun and sunscreen!´ Prue Latchford, the 2001 Australian Masters Title holder for short boarding operates the East Coast Surf School at Point Leo. Early each morning she walks the coast judging the tides, wind and wave size to determine exactly where her lessons will be conducted. `Modest and intensely private. Dedicated and professional. Caring and genuine. The most energetic person I have ever met´. That's what the locals say.

`Surfing is not just an interest or a hobby - it's a way of life´, says Prue at the start of every surf lesson. Prue is grateful to those who have helped her. `I have surfed with Phil and Paul Trigger - my extended family - for more than 30 years. They lent me boards when I had none and they still inspire me´. Prue is an example of how surfing crosses almost every socio-economic and philosophical barrier you can imagine. Her greatest satisfaction has come from working in the surf with disabled people, disadvantaged youth and multicultural groups, particularly Vietnamese, Somalian, Iraqi, Korean and Arabic. Prue believes that surfing provides a source of education and a means of personal development. It is not surprising that Prue's daily commitment to herself is to talk to a special friend or a family member every single day.

Meet Jan Duntan

LONG BOARD CHAMPION

Women of all ages are plunging into the waves. There is a whole culture around women's surfing. Jan Duntan has won the Australian Long Board Surfing titles at Bells Beach. She regards it as her greatest achievement and talks about the enormous respect it has earned from her two sons who also share Jan's love of the surf. `I dance when I am surfing with my children´.

Jan works as a surfing instructor and can often be found catching a wave between lessons. She has been described as `a friend of everyone´. Jan loves Point Leo which some fondly refer to as Trigger Point. `It's a small town where everyone knows each other and there is a strong sense of community. There are no pubs or through traffic so it is a great place for families´.

Meet Phil Trigger

TRIGGER BROS. SURFBOARDS

Queenscliff born Phil Trigger and his brother Paul grew up with a natural attraction to the ocean. Their father had given them solid timber body boards made from the centre panel of a Queen Anne dining table. The brothers soon began making their own and *Trigger Bros. Surfboards* was established in 1970. They now have seven stores.

The blanks are supplied from Queensland and the glassing and finishing are completed at Point Leo. About thirty boards per week are made over summer. Competitive surfing became the company's strength with the brothers winning Victorian Titles. Their entire staff is involved in either surfing, skating, snowboarding or sail boarding.

Phil Trigger has been surfing 4-5 days a week for the last thirty-five years. He started riding the Malibu in the mid 1980's and has competed in many State and National Titles. In recent years Phil has become a Stubby convert. These boards are made between 6'2" and 9' long and up to 3 ¾" thick. `They are so much better, easy to sink. When the wave moves over you the buoyancy can be felt thrusting you forward, sometimes rocketing you out of the water. It is not as tiring even after a three hour session´.

Asked about his relationship with his brother, Phil replied, `Co-operation was learned at an early age. When we had to walk more than two miles to surf, carrying two huge boards, it was in our best interest to carry both of them simultaneously, Paul at the front and me at the back´.

Phil doesn't smoke or drink. He has a liquid addiction of another kind and a dedication to a lifestyle. When Phil was twelve he remembers his mother's comments `salt water dissolves your brain cells´. Phil is the epitome of surfing, a man who has caught countless waves. Behind the ocean blue eyes he is a composed man with an inner calm and radiant smile. He has never changed direction. Nor has he become bored. He talks with enthusiasm about the way older guys are coming back to surfing and how mothers are learning to surf with the longer boards.

Phil Trigger with the tandem board he made for his grandson at three months of age. Corey's hand and foot prints were included left of the design.

Merricks

Merricks is an unspoiled tranquil seascape with unmade, tree-lined winding roads. It is one of the Mornington Peninsula's oldest farming areas and an established wine-growing centre.

Merricks Beach

Balnarring

Balnarring is the second largest village in the Western Port Region. Balnarring Beach was originally called Tulum, aboriginal for `black or wild duck´ that populated the nearby creek and wetlands. A feature of this unspoilt sandy beach is the early morning training of horses. Permits are required for each horse and issued subject to strict requirements. Many riders have enjoyed the sight of dolphins curious about the horses in the water. The popular television show *Neighbours* has been filmed at Balnarring Beach due to its beautiful scenery and easy access.

HMAS Cerberus

HMAS Cerberus has been the Royal Australian Navy's training establishment since 1911 training around 6000 personnel annually. In the future it will also train members of the Australian Army and Royal Australian Air Force. The facility is located on Hanns Inlet. According to Greek mythology *Cerberus* signifies the three-headed guard dog to the gates of Hades.

CERBERUS

Stony Point

Stony Point is a working port located at the end of a promontory adjacent to HMAS Cerberus Naval Establishment and the entrance to Hanns Inlet. Tugs, pilot boats and ferries are prominent. It is a popular launching place for recreational fishing and visits to French Island.

Mangroves at high tide, Stony Point

Crib Point

HMAS Otama, Crib Point Jetty

HMAS Otama is a ninety metre long Oberon-Class submarine. It was decommissioned in 2000 after 24 years in service with the navy. These submarines are being replaced with Collins-Class vessels. The motto of the Australian Submarine Service is `Stealth and Strength´. These boats go unseen and unheard in guarding Australia.

Woolleys Beach

Hastings

Hastings has developed from a fishing village to become the commercial and industrial centre of the Western Port Region. The beautiful bay and expansive foreshore reserve overlook French Island. A fascinating feature is the tidal range in excess of three metres exposing mud flats through which a boating channel winds to deep water.

The white mangroves are the most southerly in the world and are the only wooden species which live with roots inundated by salt water. Western Port is recognised as one of the world's precious areas for wading birds that make the journey from North Asia to shelter in the salt marshes and feed from the plentiful marine life.

Hastings Jetty

Woolleys Beach Reserve is located near Crib Point Jetty. It is a narrow stony beach fringed with open woodland and manna gums.

Historic Jacks Beach lies between Hastings and Crib Point. The track and boardwalk traverses the mangrove-dominated coastline for 3.5 kilometres to the boat harbour at Hastings. Jacks Beach was named after the Jack Brothers, fishermen and bark cutters who built stone tanning pits on the beach in the 1840's. Stripped bark was used in the tanning process of fishing nets.

Meet Dave Stewart & Derinda Hoyle

HASTINGS RESIDENTS

City dwellers can adapt to country living and thrive. Dave and Derinda are testimony to this. Both lived in the city until seventeen years ago when they discovered Hastings and now call it home. Hastings provided the destination for the passions that led them there. Dave is attached to the sea, Derinda to horses and land.

Both speak of Hastings with such zest and deep feeling. It has everything according to Dave, `It is very diverse - Woolleys Beach, swimming at Cannons Creek, the boardwalk at Jack's Beach, mangroves. The fishing is great here; Port Phillip Bay is too shallow. We have a marina and yacht club. If you have a boat in Hastings it is heaven´.

Dave knows all the shopkeepers and praises their great service. `If a local doesn't have the money he is told that tomorrow will be fine - this gives a sense of real humanity. They treat you like a person. The way the world is heading at the moment it is great that the Australian ethic of *no worries mate* still exists here. You would have to go to the sticks to do better. This is country ethics close to the city´.

At Derinda's home the kettle is always on. She perpetuates Hastings hospitality and loves the environment where people are not scared to be friendly. Derinda struggles to suggest a down side to the place, `Public transport especially for teenagers is lacking but even that can be a positive - we always know where our kids are because we have to drive them everywhere´. Derinda's dream for acreage has come to fruition in Hastings with a sense of belonging to a close-knit community and everything at her doorstep.

Meet Jeff Weir

DOLPHIN RESEARCH INSTITUTE

The Mornington Peninsula and Western Port Region is so significant that in 2002 the United Nations Educational Scientific and Cultural Organization (UNESCO) proclaimed it as the World's first Urban Biosphere in a coastal setting. No capital city on the planet can match Melbourne's proximity to uniquely significant marine environments. The seabed of Bass Strait is known to hold the highest density of species per square metre anywhere on land or sea.

Jeff Weir is the Executive Director of the internationally recognised Dolphin Research Institute (DRI) in Hastings. `It is fortunate that we humans care so much for dolphins because not only is their protection important as an end in itself, but like smiling ambassadors they offer us a vehicle to achieve a much greater end for the entire marine environment. By caring for dolphins we are really caring for the ocean´.

The Institute's objectives are carried out through a mix of research, education and community involvement. With a background in Marine Biology, Jeff is involved in a diverse range of activities including consulting to tourism developers, recommending legislative changes, teacher education, television documentaries, school programs, writing and public lecturing. Jeff maintains the Dolphin Research Institute is respected by government, the scientific world and the wider community because of its progressive culture. `The DRI does not complain and blame, but rather seeks to work actively and constructively with all the stakeholders in order to achieve sustainable solutions´.

`The Dolphin Research Institute runs two community programs, *I sea, I care* and *Adopt-A-Dolphin*. Inquiries are welcome on 1300 130 949´.

DOLPHIN RESEARCH INSTITUTE

Pelicans, Hastings Jetty

Western Port Bay Festival

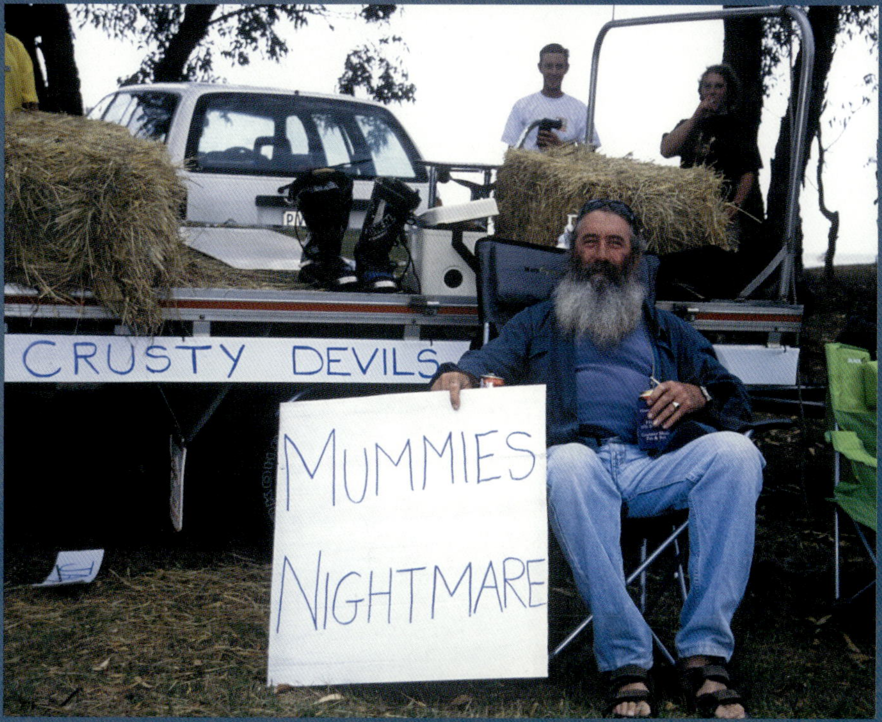
CRUSTY DEVILS
MUMMIES
NIGHTMARE

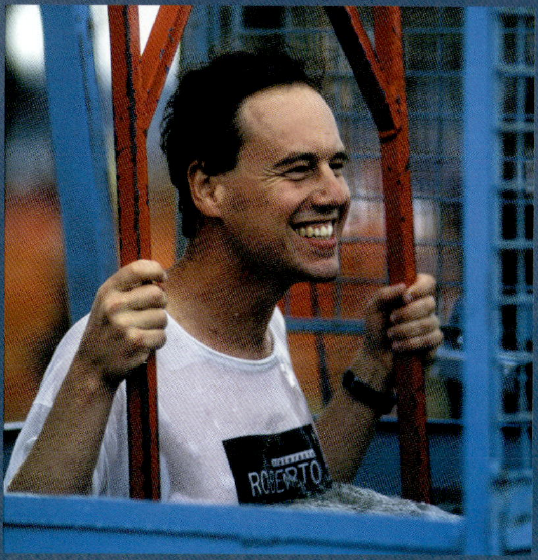

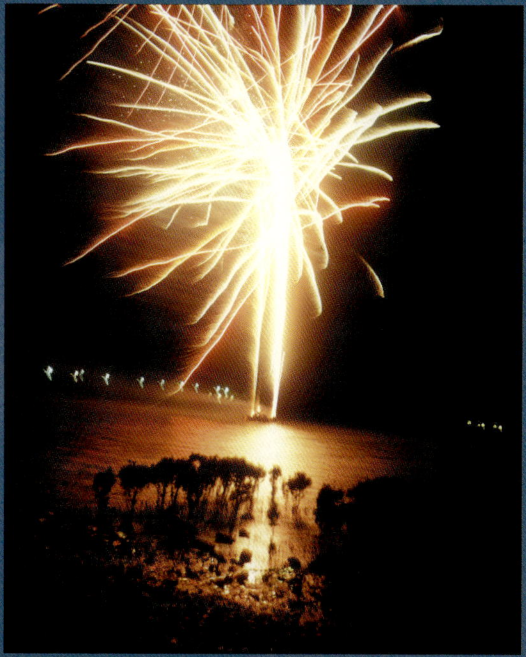

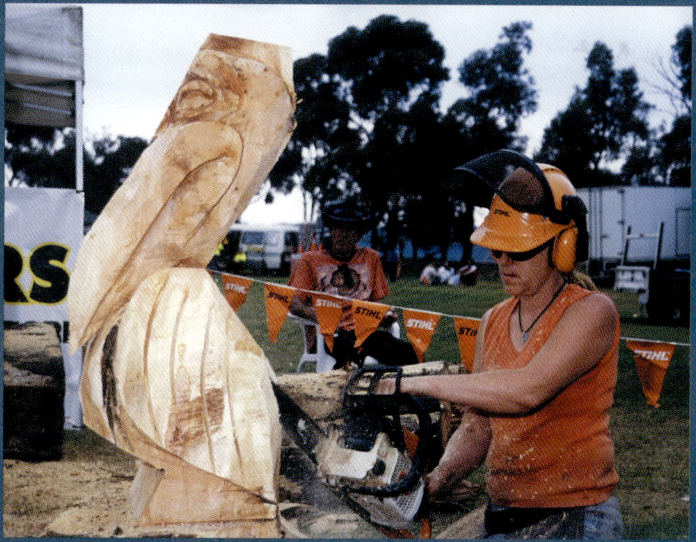
STIHL

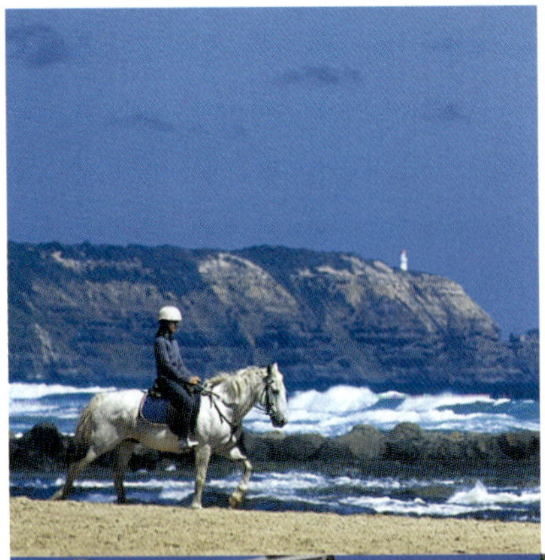
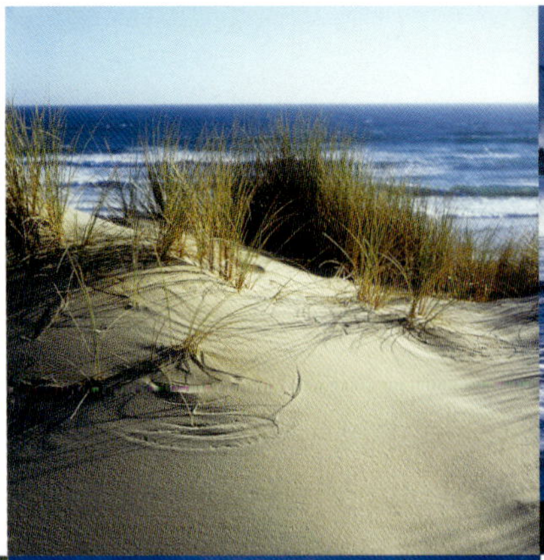
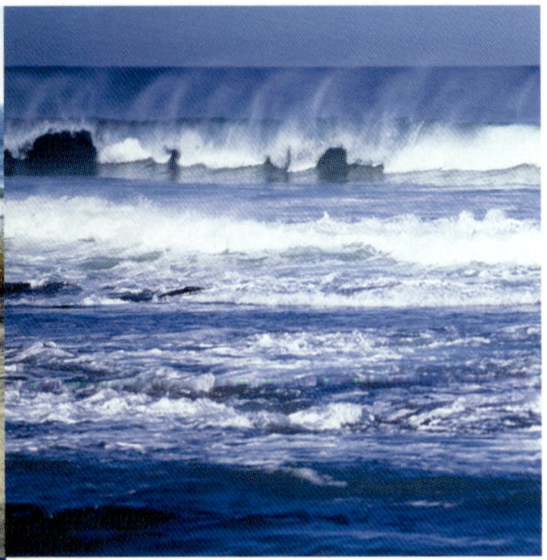
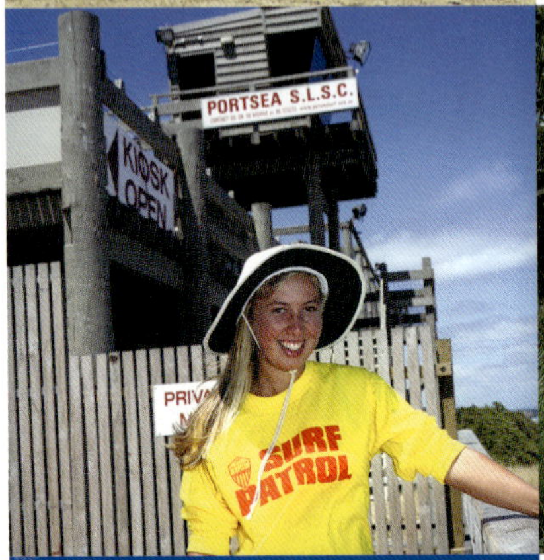
PORTSEA S.L.S.C.
KIOSK OPEN
SURF PATROL
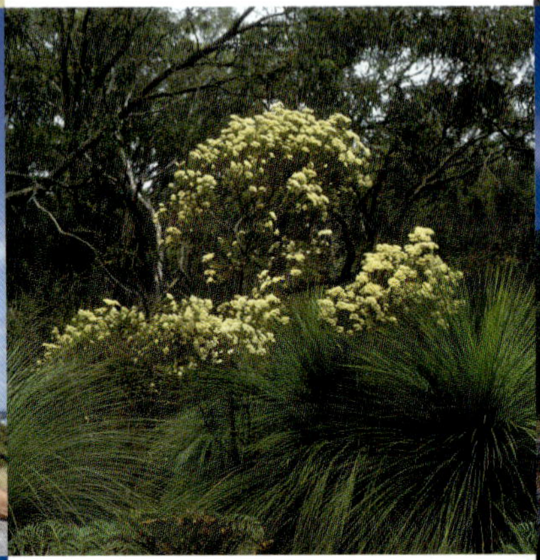
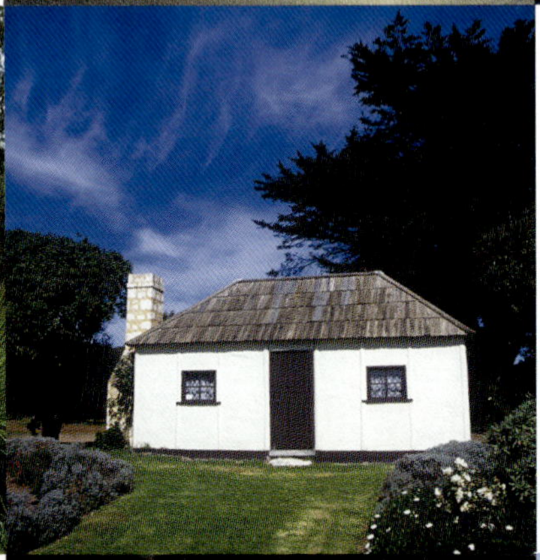
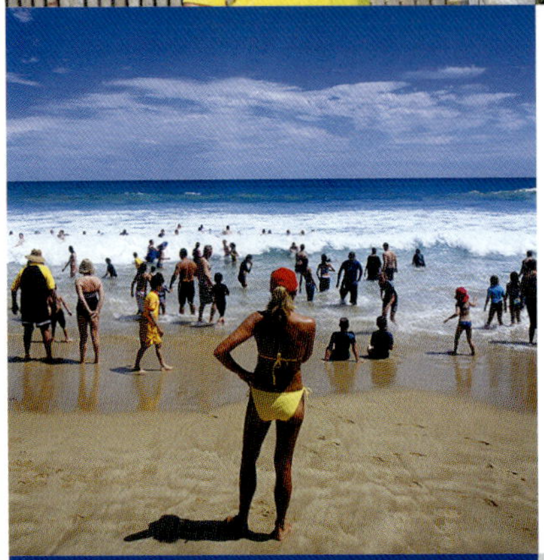
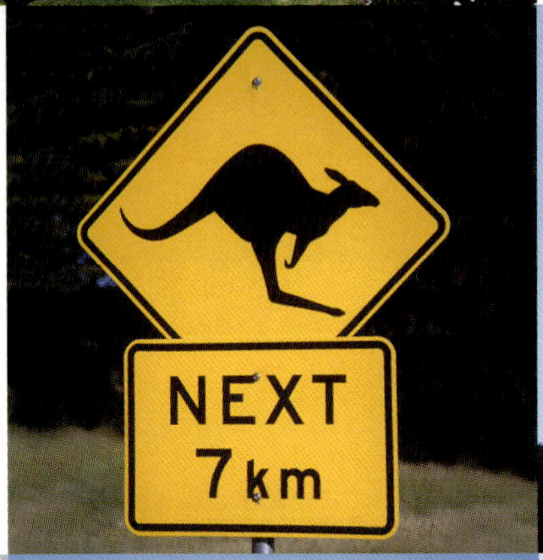
NEXT
7km
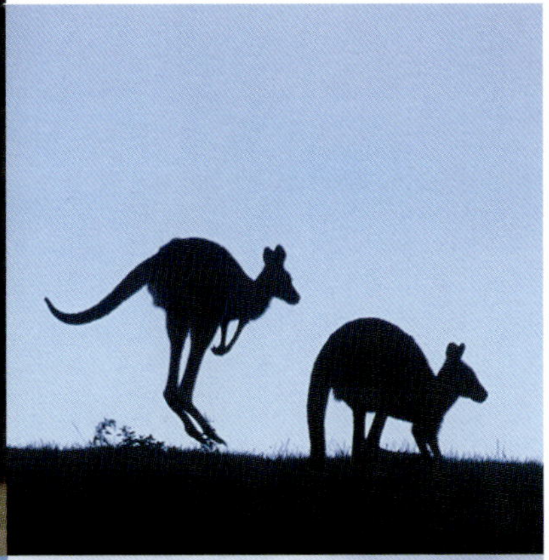
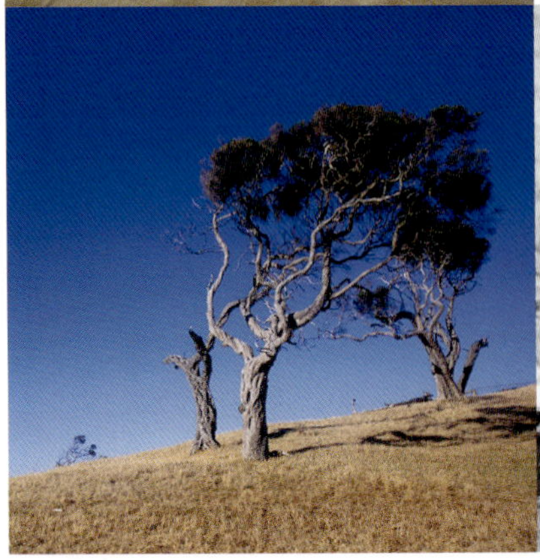
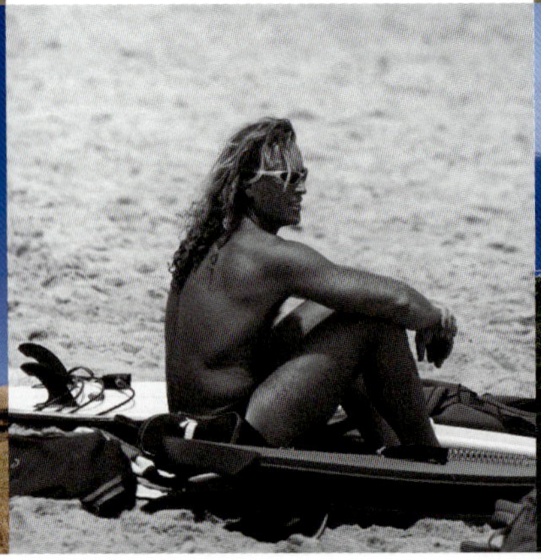
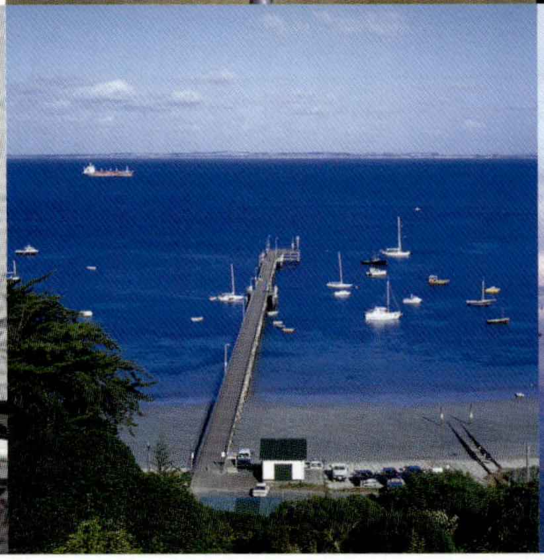
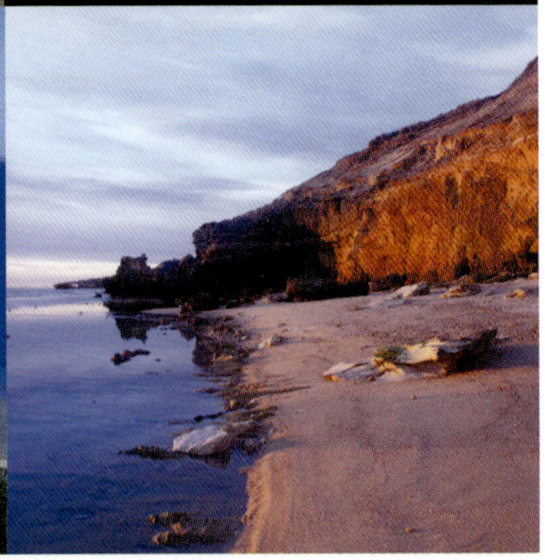

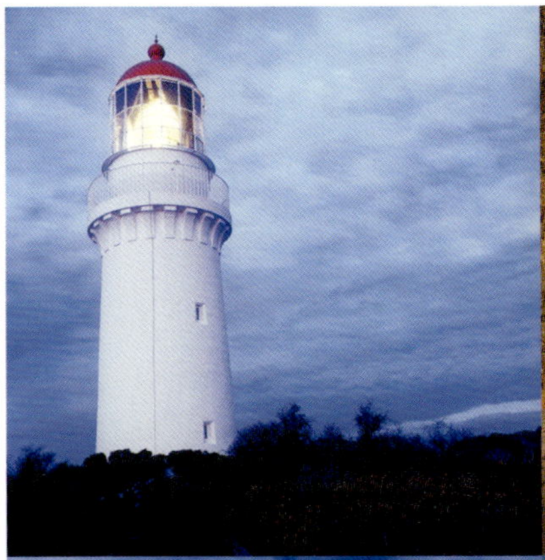
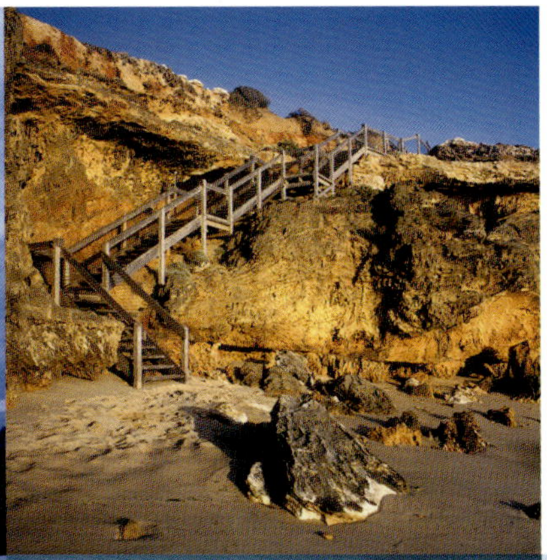
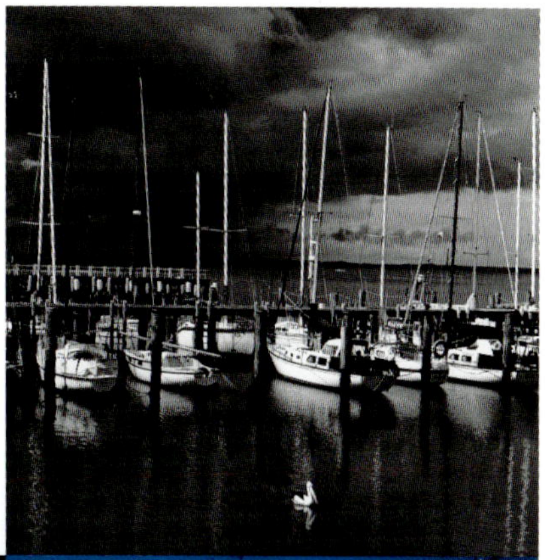
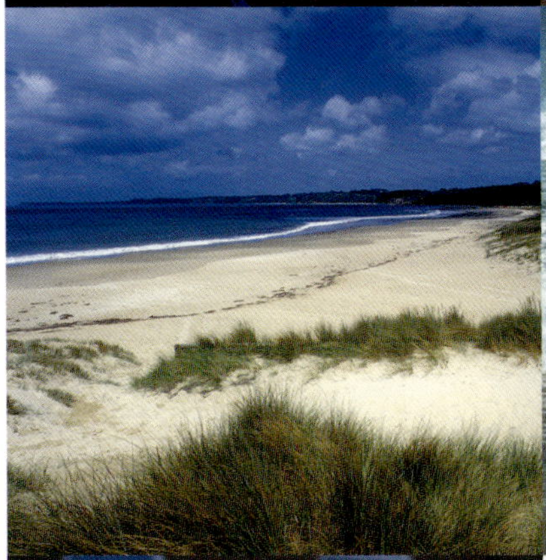
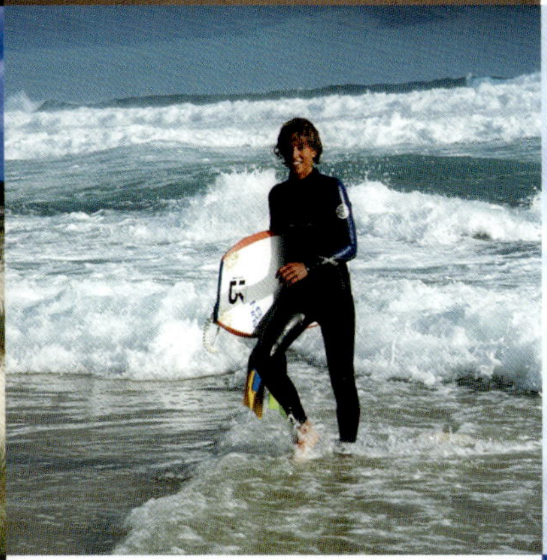
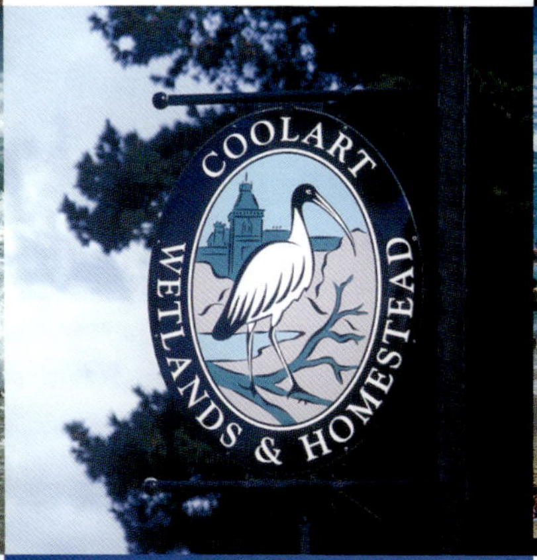
COOLART
WETLANDS & HOMESTEAD
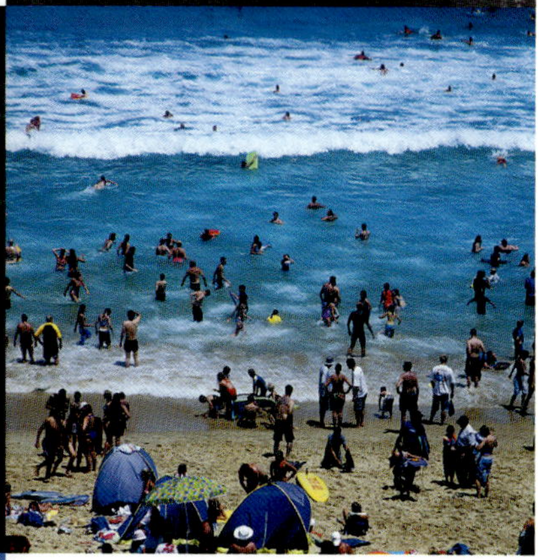
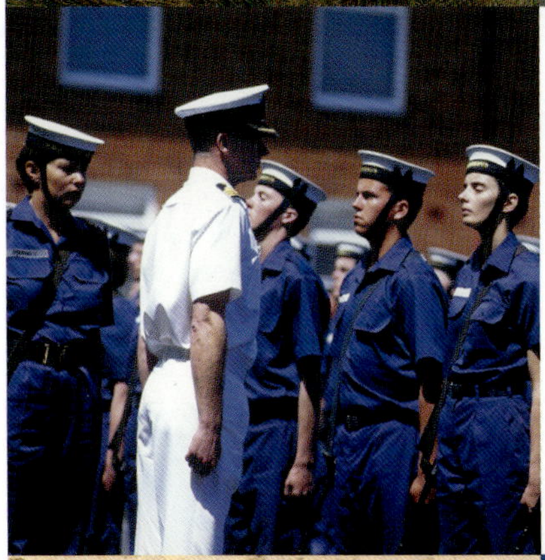
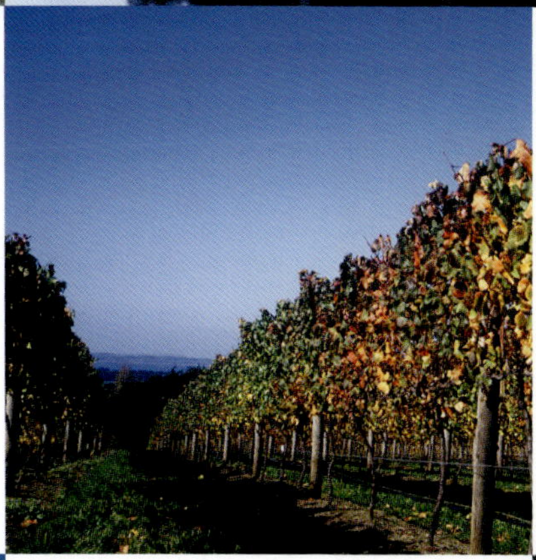
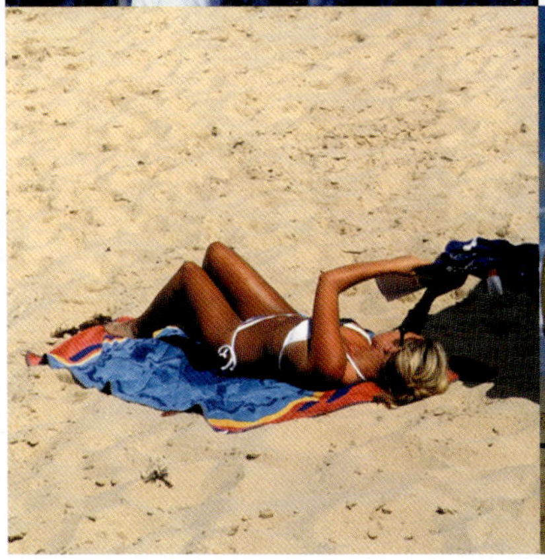
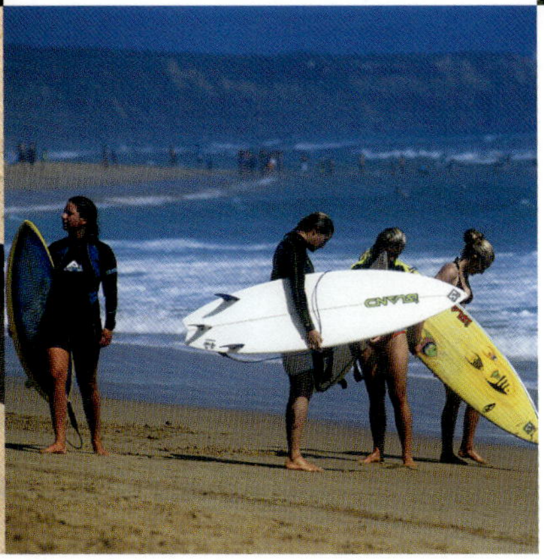
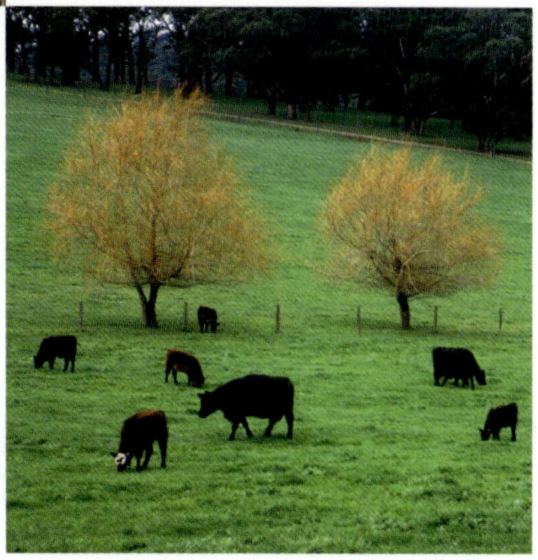

Acknowledgements

Mornington Peninsula is about place and people. We are grateful to those individuals who love the area as much as we do and who gave us their support so enthusiastically.

We would especially like to acknowledge and thank the following:
Dale Monteith, Ed Monteith, Michael Plumridge, Anna Boetta, Richard I'Anson, Andrew Mackinnon, Greg Hunt MP, Peter Charles, Patricia Kovacic, Mary Head, Andrew Taylor, Captain Charles Griffiths, Peter Friend, Phyllis Kailis, Bob Tanner, generous locals who consented to interviews and our close personal friends who provided ongoing encouragement.

Our heartfelt gratitude is extended to Dame Elisabeth Murdoch AC DBE for writing the foreword. It is a privilege to have met this remarkable lady.

Bryce Dunkley wishes to dedicate this book to his mother Rita, who sadly passed away during the production of this book. Rita's positive outlook throughout life is testimony to her philosophy that stumbling blocks can be turned into stepping stones.

Coppins Lookout, Sorrento

Published in 2003
Ides Publishing
PO BOX 201
CARNEGIE 3163
VICTORIA AUSTRALIA
Phone: (03) 9569 7169
E-mail: idespublishing@connexus.net.au

All rights reserved. No part of this publication may be reproduced, stored in a retrieval system or transmitted in any form by any means electronic, mechanical, photocopying or otherwise without the prior written permission of the publisher.

Copyright © Ides Publishing 2003

National Library of Australia
Cataloguing-in-Publication data:

Monteith Anne.
Mornington Peninsula: Sea Breeze and Sand

ISBN 0-9750912-0-4.

1. Mornington Peninsula (Vic.) - Pictorial works. I. Dunkley, Bryce Clifford. II. Title

994.52

Photography by Bryce Dunkley
Text by Anne Monteith and Bryce Dunkley
Book and cover design by David Kemp/Cthonic
E-mail: cthonic@bigpond.com

Printed and bound in China
by CTPS through
The Bookmaker
E-mail: bookmake@bigpond.net.au